CRUISE SHIP SPEAKING

How to Build a 6 Figure
Speaking Business While
Traveling the World
For Free

JOSHUA SETH

ISBN 978-0-9818472-1-4

Published By:
New You Publishing 3867 W. Market St. Suite 123 Fairlawn, OH
44333 http://www.cruiseshipspeaking.com

To Suzy, my constant companion on over 100 cruises.

Table of Contents

Introduction To Cruise Ship Speaking...7

Claim Your Free MP3 9

Are You One Of These 3 Kinds Of Speakers?...11

How I Got Started Speaking On Cruise Ships..14

Why You Should Jump At The Chance To Speak On Cruise Ships 23

Stories From The 7 Seas: Istanbul 28

What Kind Of Talks Can You Do? 31

How To Customize A Cruise Ship Lecture Based On Your Area Of Expertise ..34

How Much Can You Make 38

The 5 Step System To Six Figure Cruise Ship Speaking.....................................40

Cruise Ship Speaking On Steroids: Your Own Seminar At Sea 52

How To Get The Gigs: 5 Ways To Get Booked Now 57

Turning Free Into Fee: Types Of Bor Sales You Can Do 64

How Writing A Book Can Help Your Speaking Business 70

3 Things You Must Not Do Or Risk Walking The Plank 80

Stories From The 7 Seas: Thailand 85

Frequently Asked Questions 88

Talk the Talk: Glossary of Nautical Terminology 95

How to Pack for Your Cruise Ship Trip (Without Checking Any Luggage) 98

Can't Sleep in Hotels? Try This Travel Tip… 103

Passport Information 105

The First Step To Creating Your Six Figure Speaking Business 112

Cruise Line Contact Information 117

Stories From The 7 Seas: Italy 126

The Complete Cruise Ship Speaking System 128

About the Author 131

Cruise Ship Speaking   Joshua Seth

Introduction To Cruise Ship Speaking

Thank you for investing in *"Cruise Ship Speaking: How to Build a 6 Figure Speaking Business While Traveling the World For Free."* I have created this book to give you a quick start introduction to the wonderful world of cruise ship speaking.

Many speakers have heard that it's possible get free cruises in exchange for delivering a few presentations, but very few realize that you can use these opportunities to develop a six figure speaking business through product sales, spin-off engagements, and pre-qualified list building.

In the last few years I've been able to build my own highly profitable speaking business this way and help my coaching clients to do the same. Now these inside secrets are yours to profit from as well.

If you haven't done so already, please download and listen to the Free companion MP3 at **www.CruiseShipSpeaking.com**

And finally, make sure you take advantage of the special offer available to you at the end of this book. Although contact information for the cruise lines is provided within these pages, it's a good idea to go through the complete Cruise Ship Speaking System before you approach any of the entertainment directors.

You've only got one chance to make a first impression, so make sure you're prepared to the fullest before you do. This is a small, tight-knit industry, where everyone seems to know what everyone else is doing. As you'll see, there are only a couple of dozen cruise lines, so you don't want to risk blowing it with any of them.

By the time you've gone through the entire Cruise Ship Speaking System not only will you find it easy to make a great impression your first time out but you'll also know the inside secrets to making cruise ship speaking highly profitable and extraordinarily fun.

So let's get started...It's time to trade airports for islands, boring hotel rooms for floating state rooms, and dimly lit conference rooms for cruise ship decks drenched in the sun of an endless summer :-)

Let me be the first to say "welcome aboard!"

Joshua Seth
www.cruiseshipspeaking.com

Claim Your Free MP3

As a special bonus for investing in this book I'd like to give you access to an interview I did recently on how to become a cruise ship speaker. It's jammed packed with information on the subject and will really enhance the value of the book you now hold in your hands. Simply go to **www.CruiseShipSpeaking.com** to claim your free copy.

You'll Discover:

- How much demand there really is for you to speak on cruise ships
- Why speaking on cruise ships is actually better (and easier) than many traditional speaking venues
- How anybody can take their speaking topic and make it match what the cruise ships are looking for
- How speaking on cruise ships is one of the fastest and easiest ways to get a killer demo (showing you on a big stage in front of huge audiences).
- The one person you need to impress so you can get rebooked again and again (piss this person off and your days of free cruising are over!)
- Where you can go and what you can do... for free!

- What you'll need to know before you go
- Why you'll want to get started right away
- The secret of how to make money forever from your cruise talks

Claim Your Free Bonus MP3 at
www.CruiseShipSpeaking.com

Are You One Of These 3 Kinds Of Speakers?

I've written this book for three types of speakers:

1. Speakers who would like to get booked on cruise ships

2. Speakers who already do cruise ship lecturing but want to learn how to make these gigs incredibly profitable

3. Variety entertainers (magicians, hypnotists, and comics) who perform on cruise ships and want to add speaking and product sales to their onboard shows so they can double or triple their income.

It is my sincere desire that the ideas presented within these pages will help you both to get booked speaking on cruise ships as well as to understand how to use those talks to develop a six figure speaking business.

When I started on cruise ships, it was as a guest entertainer. I did my stage hypnosis shows and that was it. The cruise line paid me handsomely for the opportunity to perform in a beautiful 1,000 seat theater for one night of the voyage and also provided me and my wife Suzy with an all expense paid vacation to exotic ports of call all over the world.

That, in and of itself, was awesome. But it wasn't until I started adding a 1 hour lecture and some product sales to my time spent on board that I began to understand how much more profitable these gigs could be.

There's nothing wrong with wanting to speak on cruise ships simply so you can get free vacations. That's a great place to start. But you're leaving the lion's share of the profits on the table if that's all you think there is to this opportunity.

Cruise ship speaking can be used to build yourself a stable, six figure speaking business when you know how to really work the system. And that's exactly what I want to show you how to do.

Most speakers have heard about speaking on cruise ships but have absolutely no idea how to go about getting booked to do it. Even if they do they have no idea how to turn these engagements into highly profitable endeavors.

Throughout this book I'll be showing you how you can get booked to speak on cruise ships, do it the right way so you can travel for free for the rest of your life, and use these opportunities to make some serious money and build your own six figure speaking business in the process.

Joshua Seth doing an
onboard lecture
to a packed house

A NOTE TO ENTERTAINERS:

Cruise ships provide a great venue for your talents and can provide you with a lot of work. You make a few grand a week, get to travel the world, and can add "internationally touring act" to your resume. But what happens when you get back on land?

If you do enough cruise ship contracts you'll soon find that people forget about you back home. You'd better have a way to build your business back on land even when you're at sea or all the other work will dry up in your absence.

Speaking is the answer to this problem. If you've never given a lecture before, just know that it's like doing a really simple show, with no music or lighting cues. Even something as simple as a magician adding a magic class and how to DVD to his onboard offerings has the potential to both sell a lot of products on board the vessel and build a list of clients and customers for his business back home. It's easy, it's profitable, and it's fun. Keep reading and I'll show you how.

Doing my show to a packed house of about a thousand people in the main shipboard theater

How I Got Started Speaking On Cruise Ships

The year was 2005 and I was slowly killing myself.

Not literally of course, but it felt that way. I was living in spartan hotel rooms, noisy airports, and bland conference rooms. This is what most speakers consider "successful".

Hah! It was driving me crazy.

I loved sharing my message in front of an audience of course. Whether presenting or performing there is still nothing more exciting than stepping onto a platform with a mic in your hand and creating an unforgettable shared experience.

But spending your life going after gigs all the time, endlessly marketing to meeting planners, getting stuck in airports and in traffic, and stressing out on the way to the venue? I'd had enough of that.

Yes, I was making a great living, but I was working waaaay too hard to enjoy it. Then I discovered a speaking market that literally gave me my life back... cruise ships!

CRUISE SHIPS GAVE ME MY LIFE BACK

In the last few years my wife and I have been able to take over 100 cruises, to exotic destinations all over the world, typically working just 3 hours a week, and getting paid big money to do it.

We have travelled *for free* to:

- The Caribbean
- The Mediterranean
- Every island in Hawaii
- Tahiti, Moorea, and Bora Bora
- Alaska and the Inside Passage
- Brazil
- Singapore
- Thailand
- England
- Ireland
- France
- Belgium
- Norway
- Denmark
- Bermuda
- Jamaica
- Belize
- Columbia
- The Bahamas
- Both coasts of Mexico
- All over Central and South America
- Costa Rica
- The Panama Canal
- Australia and New Zealand
- Italy
- Spain
- Turkey
- Monaco
- The Greek Isles
- And many more exotic destinations.

All that travel and adventure would have normally cost us hundreds of thousands of dollars, but as a guest of the cruise lines we've done it all for free.

Not only that, but the 3 hours of "work" I trade for this amazing lifestyle are some of the most fun and rewarding experiences I've ever had in my life. Why work so hard going after the same speaking markets everybody else does when cruise ships offer such low hanging fruit?

REAL SUCCESS = FREEDOM

I didn't know that this lifestyle was even possible or I would have done it years ago. My wife Suzy and I have been speaking and performing on cruise ships for years now and have taken over 100 cruises.

Before I started in this market I used to live in Los Angeles being "successful". Which in this business means flying all over the place, living out of hotel rooms, and always on the phone and the email with clients, trying to book one gig after the other.

Be careful what you ask for in this business. You become successful, and then you become very busy, and then you start to lose the quality of your life. That scenario didn't make sense to me.

So I made a big change. I decided to make life an exciting adventure and travel the world, have somebody else pay for it, and work two or three hours a week.

I'm actually only contracted for two hours a week as a guest entertainer, but I like to throw in that extra third hour as an enrichment lecturer because I can make more from speaking in that third hour than I do from performing in the first two!

Cruise Ship Speaking Joshua Seth

MY FIRST BOOKING

So what happened was, I got booked on my first cruise strictly as a guest entertainer. I went though an agent instead of submitting directly to the cruise line. Agents can be great for entertainers, but speakers should really deal with the cruise lines directly. More on that later.

The very first time you give a presentation onboard the ship you're going to be evaluated and if you do well you'll get offered a lot more cruising opportunities. If you don't, you can kiss this market goodbye. That's why you want to be really well prepared before you approach either an agent or a cruise line in the first place. You've got one shot at this. Make it count.

That first cruise ship gig was nearly four years ago now and seems like a distant memory. I didn't have a book like this to refer to before my first voyage, so while it was exciting, it was also extremely confusing.

Sailors have their own terminology and I didn't know what they were talking about half the time. Nobody bothered to tell me what was expected so I had to figure things out as I went along. Also, I didn't really understand how to monetize the experience at the time, but I could tell there was a lot of potential there.

Sure, I was getting paid for the gig, but it wasn't nearly as profitable as it is right now or as much as you'll be generating after you go through my training. Still, it was enough to let me know that there was a better way.

Over the course of the first year I learned the lingo, figured out the seagoing system, and tested various BOR (product sales) strategies until I figured out what worked, what didn't, and why. Testing all the time.

Over the second year I refined the implementation of those strategies that proved successful and eliminated those that weren't. Now, after over 100 cruises, I can literally walk onto a ship anywhere in the world and generate a ton of spin-off bookings and product sales every single time. It's really very exciting.

How This System Evolved

The cruise line hires me to do my comedy hypnosis stage show aboard the world's biggest cruise ships while my wife and I get to travel to exotic far off lands. It's a great gig. We typically perform in a beautiful theater in front of 2,000 people (over the course of two shows) on one night per cruise.

The rest of our time on board is free to enjoy the vacation just like any other passenger. The only difference is I get paid thousands of dollars to take the voyage. Like I said, it's not a bad gig.

After every show, people come up to me and ask if I can help them lose weight. Lots of people ask me this, partially because I'm a hypnotist and weight loss is one of the most well known uses of hypnosis, and partially because the average weight gain on a 7 day cruise is eight pounds!

I've got what they want...a way to lose all the weight they just gained. They've got a problem and they're coming to me for the solution.

Your Message To Market Match

When you find a solid connection between what you're offering and what the buying public is asking for that is called having a great message to market match. And that is exactly the situation in which I found myself.

1. They know I'm a hypnotist
2. They just gained a bunch of weight
3. They want me to help them lose the weight with hypnosis

Result: message to market match.

In this situation I don't have to do any selling at all, just schedule an appointment. Problem is I don't do one on one hypnosis sessions anymore. Why charge people a couple hundred bucks for one hypnosis session when they can invest in my package of six weight loss hypnosis CDs and listen to them over and over again for less than the cost of a single appointment? The hypnosis CDs make a lot more sense for the consumer and they make a lot more sense for me since I'd rather spend my time traveling than sitting in a hypnosis office all day.

But people rarely buy this way (unless the product is inexpensive enough to be considered an impulse buy). Those prospects just met me. They're probably not going to plunk down a couple hundred bucks on a whole weight loss system without some more information.

They have questions. How does hypnosis work for weight loss? How will I know it will work for me? What will I need to do? Has it worked for other people in my situation? Until these questions and implied objections are answered there is buying resistance that needs to be overcome in order to make the sale. They want what I've got but they're afraid of making a mistake and so avoid making a purchasing decision.

SO WHAT DID I DO?

I started delivering educational "enrichment" lectures on the topic aboard the ship and offering my CDs afterward. It worked out great, by the end of the talk all of their questions and concerns had been answered and I was able to help the maximum number of people in the minimum amount of time.

So now I've got this talk that educates the passengers about the benefits of hypnosis for weight loss and the effectiveness of my 6 CD system and I've got a product to sell instead of my time. I'm in business!

Initially I just had a single CD by the way. That's how everyone starts off, with a single talk or a single show or a single product. Over time though I expanded my weight loss hypnosis CD into a 6 CD package, a book, and about 14 other CDs on related topics.

I've discovered which packages and bonuses and price points result in the greatest profits both on board and over the internet afterward. That's because I also use these audiences to build a database of prospects for my online automated marketing system.

The key to doing this is to offer your audience something they want, that has intrinsic value, and give it away for free (just like I'm doing now by giving you the bonus CD at www.cruiseshipspeaking.com).

Once they're on your list you can continue to offer them products and live appearance opportunities for as long as you want. The best thing about this approach to list building is that your prospects already know, like, and trust you. If they didn't, they've wouldn't have signed up for your giveaway after the talk. People like to buy from people they know, like and trust so who do you think they'll call or recommend when their company is planning it's next big event? That's right, you!

AN UNTAPPED OPPORTUNITY

Most speakers just look at cruise ships as a way to get free vacations and miss the opportunity to use them as business building profit centers.

As a result, it's a market that's totally overlooked by a most professional speakers. They think "if you can't make it in the real business then you go speak or perform on a cruise ship." Let me tell you, nothing could be further from the truth.

In addition to all the free travel and amazing experiences, I've actually been able to use the contacts I've made from these speaking engagements to build a huge list for my own shows, speaking engagements, seminars, and back end products.

I've also sold an amazing amount of CDs, DVDs, and books at the back of the room and in the gift shop while on board. As a direct result of the presentations I've given on cruise ships, I now have a six figure speaking business that pretty much runs on autopilot. No more marketing for gigs, no more "feast or famine" booking seasons. I have a stable business. And after you fully implement the strategies outlined in this book so will you.

On a personal note, I think it's important to mention that this isn't all about the money. The lifestyle you'll enjoy with your spouse or traveling companion can be just as important. My wife Suzy and I can tell you that our lives are richer and our marriage stronger for having had countless amazing life experiences together all over the world. And all from speaking on cruise ships :-)

Until now I've jealously guarded the valuable information contained within this book, happy to let everyone think there's no money to be made speaking on cruise ships, that it's just about getting free cruises and nothing more. Only my private coaching clients had access to this life changing information. But the truth of the matter is there's so many cruise ships and so much opportunity out there that there's more than enough work to go around. Some it could be yours.

Today I am committed to showing other speakers and entertainers how to profit from these amazing opportunities at sea and build their own six figure speaking businesses in the process. The result is the book you now hold in your hands.

Old Town from the top of a fort in San Juan, Puerto Rico

Cruising the Inside Passage in Alaska

Why You Should Jump At The Chance To Speak On Cruise Ships

Imagine speaking in some of the most beautiful theaters and showrooms anywhere in the world, with packed audiences and full tech support.

In traditional speaking venues, bad sound systems, impossible room set-ups, and nonexistent lighting is the norm. When you speak on cruise ships, if you want special lighting, audio visual support, even mic runners, there's a whole team of professionals ready and willing to make you look great.

In traditional speaking venues, you have to warm up the audience and get them on your side. On cruise ships your audiences are packed with smiling, happy faces.

In traditional speaking venues, you can rarely sell your books and CDs after your talks, cutting out a huge source of revenue. Not only are cruise lines happy to let you sell your books and CDs after your presentations, they'll even carry them in their gift shop, and set up an autograph table for you. And they'll even process the payments for you so you can get back to having fun in the sun!

Here are a few other benefits you'll enjoy as a cruise ship speaker:

You can get professional promo photos taken for free by the shipboard photographers

On the formal dress up nights you'll see photographers out in force all over the ship. They'll be standing in front of various lighting and background setups attempting to entice as many passengers as possible to get souvenir photos taken.

Some of these backgrounds are simple color themes like blue, black, and white. Get your promo pictures taken in front of these and then head down to the photography lab in the crew area to get deeply discounted (or even free) prints. They will look every bit as good as professionally shot photos without having to pay the session fee.

You can shoot a demo tape in front of a huge audience at one of your talks

The cruise lines already have video systems set up in the rooms where you'll be giving your presentations, so it's just a matter of taping the talk. The trick is getting them to record the tape in the first place. You can give a videotape and ten bucks to the guy in the sound booth to record your presentation for you. You can also simply bring your own video camera into the back of the room and ask your traveling companion to tape it for you. It'll be better if it's on their house system in the ceiling but you can have your own camera running as a backup.

That demo video's going to be worth it's weight in gold to you because how often are you in front of hundreds or thousands of people in such a professional-looking venue, with lights and sound and everything?

If you do want to be a corporate speaker and you haven't been in a big enough venue to get that sort of a look, with a big screen behind you and a huge audience in front of you, then this is your chance. It can look like you're presenting at a giant conference. And with that kind of a demo tape eventually you will.

You can book spin-off gigs from members of your audience

You will come into contact with thousands of people on every cruise you take. Many of them work for companies that can book you. By collecting their contact information and following up with them back on land you can develop a healthy stream of additional speaking engagements and increased revenue opportunities.

You can build a list in the thousands to market your products and services

Those same passengers will be in a position to purchase your books, CDs, and DVDs when they are back on land. In addition to generating coaching and speaking work, these prospects can continue investing in your products for years. The key is to build a list of the people in your audiences and continue to stay in light contact with them over time. I'll show you how to automate that process and do it right.

You can use all the free time to write your own book

You'll have so much free time on your cruise ship speaking gigs that you can use it to develop new products you might not have a chance to work on when you're back on land. I wrote my first book on ships and you can too. A cruise ship is the ideal place to focus on completing a major project like that and the rewards can last a lifetime.

You can get big discounts all over the ship

You can get big discounts on just about everything on the ship when you know how to work the system. I'm not going to go into detail about that here as there really are a lot of areas to cover: the gift shop, the bar, the internet access, the phones, the shore excursions, the watches and jewelry, the alcohol, to name but a few. It's beyond the scope and focus of this book, but I do want you to know that's possible to work all sorts of discounts and freebees all over the place.

Here's an example: once or twice a cruise the crew has what they call a "camboosa" sale. It's usually late at night, after the shops have closed and the passengers have turned in for the night. They open up the shops to the crew and slash prices on everything by as much as 50%. That includes the big stuff such as jewelry and watches. I was able to get a Tag Heuer timepiece at one of these sales for over $1,000 off!

You have to know what a "camboosa" sale is to take advantage of it though (which is why I'm mentioning it here). It's not like like they announce it over the speakers up on deck or anything. You typically have to go down to the crew office at the beginning of the voyage and look at the postings on the wall to find out when it will be.

All the food and non-stop entertainment you can consume

It's like living a perpetual paid vacation. Imagine never having to prepare a meal or do dishes or make your bed for that matter. Simply step out your cabin door and a world of non-stop food, fun, and adventure await.

You can travel the world for free!

As a cruise ship speaker you will get to go places and have experiences that will enrich your life. You will be exposed to other cultures, languages, and cuisines. You will expand your horizons. And you will become a more fascinating person in the process.

Swimming with the dolphins in Puerto Vallarta, Mexico

Snorkeling in Tahiti

Stories From
The 7 Seas: Istanbul

As soon as I looked out of my cabin window this morning I knew that this port would finally provide the taste of old Europe that I'd yet to find on this voyage. Mosques and minarets dotted the landscape and bright red flags with the Muslin moon and star snapped briskly in the sea breeze. It was about 90 degrees already and it was only 8am.

The first stop of the day was at the Hippodrome, the site of chariot races in old Constantinople that attracted crowds of 100,000 people. The Egyptian obelisk that still stands at it's center is over 3,500 years old and I suddenly realized that I'd never before seen anything older than a few hundred years that wasn't locked up behind glass in a museum. This massive sculpture was standing right out in the open, just steps away from the equally impressive Blue Mosque.

Men are forbidden to enter mosques with their knees exposed in Turkey and this is why I was now sweltering uncomfortably in my jeans as the temperature topped 100 degrees. It was worth it though, as again I'd never seen anything like it, not just in terms of size and age but in detailed adornment too. I took a great many pictures of the same domes and columns, trying to stitch together some semblance of the scope of the place.

Afterwards I went to a rug making demonstration which was actually quite a bit more interesting than I'd anticipated, and not just because the place was air conditioned!

Mustachioed men kept throwing rugs out onto the floor, one after another, bam bam bam, for about 45 minutes, saying as each one unrolled "This rug took 4 years to make. It's silk on silk. All hand woven". Bam! "This one took 5 years to make. It has over 600 stitches per square inch and is over 100 years old." Bam! And they'd throw another one on top of that until there were dozens of carpets piled all over each other, covering the floor completely.

Finally I entered the Grand Bazaar, home to over 7,000 shops and easily twice that many merchants trying to aggressively coerce passersby into sampling their wares. I used various accents and attitudes with the vendors and had a great time pretending to be from different parts of the world. I even posed as a Turk several times and tried to outsell the shop's vendor, enticing the tourists in with Borat like enthusiasm. It was great fun.

Eventually I just dropped my Turkish accent and did a flat out Borat impersonation. I'm sure the Turks don't know who Borat is but they loved it just the same and invited me back behind the counter for green apple tea and Turkish delights.

I got lost in the bazaar for hours and picked up a few oddities, like a bookmark made of woven Turkish carpet and a bunch of "evil eyes".

When it was time to go back to the ship, it took me nearly half an hour to figure a way out of the bazaar and back to the street where I'd started! I'd gotten entirely turned around in the never-ending maze of merchants and only managed to find my way back again because I'd noticed the particular design on the ceiling where I'd entered.

It was an exciting adventure! I highly recommend getting lost every once in a while. It's a great way to find yourself.

Cruising can be about so much more than the destinations.

Entering the port of Istanbul, Turkey

The Grand Bazaar in Istanbul, Turkey

At St. Sophia in Istanbul, Turkey. Just down the street from the stunning Blue Mosque.

Cruise Ship Speaking   Joshua Seth

What Kind Of
Talks Can You Do?

The cruise lines are primarily interested in destination lectures. However, a lot of their best cruisers have gone on these voyages over and over. So they don't want the same kind of talk. That's why there's really a huge opportunity right now. Because they don't want the same talks every time. They want your unique angle, your unique spin on things.

There are typically several port days on a single cruise though and you won't have to deliver a destination lecture on all of them. This gives you an opportunity to deliver your normal talk or develop a new one. In the next section I'll show you how to create a destination lecture that meshes with your existing area of expertise.

As a hypnotist many passengers ask me about how to lose weight with hypnosis. I have presented an enrichment lecture on this topic nearly 100 times on ships and it never fails to draw a capacity crowd of several hundred passengers. Of course, it helps that the average cruiser gains about 8 pounds on a 7 day voyage. As a result, there is a definite need among cruisers to learn how to take off the weight that they just put on.

Even though I was originally hired as a guest entertainer, I figured out pretty quickly that by adding enrichment lectures and offering products for sale afterward, not only could I help a lot of people, but I could also earn quite a bit more money on each voyage.

An enrichment lecturer is of course different from an entertainer, but I decided to become both because the enrichment lecturers have a pretty good deal.

Most of the time the cruise line will want you to talk about the destinations that you'll be sailing to, but there's still plenty of opportunity to talk about whatever you want during your other lectures.

I've done cruise ship enrichment talks in the following areas:
• Accelerated learning
• How to hypnotize
• How to overcome phobias
• How to write your own book
• How to create your own website
• Memory improvement
• Stress reduction
• Smoking cessation
• Time management
• Weight loss hypnosis

And probably a few other topics as well. Not all on the same cruise of course :-)

Why would I lecture on so many different topics by the way? Can you guess?

Well for one, every time you put together a new lecture topic you have another talk you can promote back on land. I also speak to corporate and collegiate groups a lot. Both markets are interested in accelerated learning and memory improvement techniques.

Another reason to keep coming up with new talks is that in most cases you can record your presentations and turn them into products. I don't market the time management talk for instance, but I do offer a DVD of the content at my website (www.joshuaseth.com/store) and people buy it all the time.

This product grew out of a talk I developed and delivered on a cruise ship several years ago and it's still providing some nice passive income to this very day! How cool is that huh?

At the Mendenhall Glacier in Juneau, Alaska

How To Customize
A Cruise Ship Lecture
Based On Your
Area Of Expertise

The number one most popular topic the cruise lines are looking for is a destination talk. In other words, a presentation about the port or general area where the ship is sailing. There's a catch though: because so many passengers are repeat cruisers, they want a unique approach to the subject matter. If the destination lecture was taken straight out of a guide book chances are most people in the audience would be bored to tears.

This situation creates a great opportunity for you.

If your area of expertise is something other than the region you're sailing to you can creatively combine the two topics into a unique lecture presentation. Let me give you a couple of examples.

Let's say you're a motivational speaker and you want to get booked on a cruise ship through the Panama Canal. Well the man who built the Panama Canal, John Frank Stevens, had to motivate hundreds of demoralized and disillusioned workers that this job could in fact be done. He also had to motivate Congress to fund his vision. And if that weren't enough, he had to motivate scores of railroad workers to head down to the jungle, despite news of sickness and death, and complete the work on the project. He succeeded "and today we have the marvel of human engineering that everyone aboard will get a chance to experience today."

Do you see how easy it is to wrap your speaking topic around the ship's destination? I hope so. You can do this with just about any topic too.

Let's say your area of expertise is leadership, you could use the same example above and simply change the focus. Or you could center the narrative around President Theodore Roosevelt and how great leaders leave a lasting legacy (such as the Panama Canal) for future generations.

If you're a health and wellness speaker you could lecture on the topic of malaria and yellow fever and how eradicating it was a key to the success of the building of the canal.

Just about any speaking topic can be combined with a geographic region and a knowledge of history to create a unique and compelling destination lecture.

You're going to want to prepare more than one talk but, it doesn't need to take you very long to create these lectures. I've outlined enrichment lectures on the plane or even on the day of the event. They only need to be up to an hour long and presumably you already know your subject area, so it's just a matter of coming up with a unique angle that will tie into the cruise and be of interest to the passengers.

On a recent cruise I saw an enrichment lecturer doing a series of talks on celebrity murders, which has nothing to do with any particular port. They were Hollywood stories, like the O. J. Simpson story and Robert Blake. And you know what? His talks were so well attended that they put him in that big theater where I do my shows. That's a thousand-seat theater, and there wasn't an empty seat in the house.

On another cruise I took recently, I saw a very interesting two-part talk. This speaker was actually able to fill two different enrichment slots based on the life of the great master magician Houdini. Passengers of all ages attended and absolutely loved it.

Another example would be famous places around the world, because obviously these are people that are interested in traveling, and it doesn't necessarily always have to be about the specific places that will be visited on that voyage. In fact, the cruise lines seem to like talks about far flung ports of call because then you're getting the audience intrigued about taking more cruises to other parts of the world.

It's also a good idea to have an extra talk ready to go in case of emergency. Occasionally the ship will miss the port and you'll end up with an unexpected sea day. This can actually turn out quite well for you though as you'll have a chance to impress the cruise director and an extra opportunity to promote your products after your lecture.

On a recent cruise from New York, we were scheduled to stop in Bermuda and couldn't because of wind and high seas. Bermuda can be notoriously windy and several times I have been on ships that have been unable to dock once they've sailed to that island because of the weather. Actually, this just happened a few of weeks ago in England too, when we were sailing from Le Havre, France. The ship couldn't stop because of the wind.

On days like these, you wake up in the morning all ready to go to shore and have an adventure. And then you hear, "Bong-bong-bong, this is your captain speaking. I regret to inform you that we will not be docking in port today due to high waves and strong wind. We take your safety seriously as our first concern, and we are sorry for the inconvenience, and hope you will have a wonderful day on the ship."

What happens when you hear that announcement is that the cruise director, the head of your department, is freaking out. He has to figure out how to fill an entire day's worth of activities. So you want to have an extra talk already set to go. Then you can saunter down to the cruise director's office in the morning and say, "Hey, I heard we're going to miss the port today. By the way, would it be helpful for you if I gave an extra lecture on topic XYZ?"

You're going to be his best friend that day. You're also likely to get a great review at the end of that cruise as well :-)

How Much Can You Make

In addition to all the free travel, adventure abroad, and list building opportunities, there is of course the little matter of your fee.

If you're a guest entertainer, then you'll most likely make between $2,500 and $3,500 per voyage. That's the going rate at the time of this writing. If you're strictly an enrichment lecturer though, you won't get paid anything by the cruise line.

That's right, they won't pay you a dime. But not to worry, there are plenty of other ways to make cruise ship speaking a profitable launching pad for your six figure speaking business.

"Wait a second, what about my speaking fee?"

This is a big concern for a lot of speakers. They seem to think that if they don't get a check at the end of their speech that they didn't make a profit. Of course, nothing could be further from the truth. There are many ways to make a speech profitable, sometimes more profitable than if you'd been paid directly for giving it.

True, you won't be getting an upfront fee as a cruise ship speaker, but you will be getting a cruise for two worth thousands of dollars. If you think of this arrangement in terms of the barter system then that's a fair trade for most speakers.

But it doesn't stop there, you are also allowed (even encouraged) to sell books, CDs, and DVDs after your talks. Do this right and you can generate thousands of dollars of additional revenue on each cruise you take. Most speakers do an exceedingly poor job of this however, and end up selling a few hundred dollars worth of product at best.

The key is to offer more than one product, make them relevant to your area of expertise and of interest to the passengers, and then bundle them together in a package deal that makes every sale much more profitable for you and a great bargain for the people getting it.

Watch the Big BOR DVD in the complete Cruise Ship Speaking System a couple of times before you take your first cruise and see exactly how I do it. Not to brag, but I have yet to see another cruise ship speaker outsell me after a talk.

I don't push or use any high-pressure tactics (that would be a good way to burn your bridges in this market). I do offer great content at a fair price that a lot of passengers take advantage of at the conclusion of my presentation. You can do this too and it can result in thousands of dollars worth of product sales on every voyage. Just remember, all sales go through the gift shop and nothing should be sold directly for cash.

Refer to the full Cruise Ship Speaking System for extensive coverage of this topic.

The 5 Step System To Six Figure Cruise Ship Speaking

Whenever I work with my coaching clients on achieving a big goal (like writing a book, creating a marketing plan, or entering a new speaking market) I always like to break things down into manageable steps.

The five steps I've outlined below can't be taken all at once. One necessarily needs to follow the other. But once you've taken all of them you'll have built a six figure speaking business that can provide you with security and prosperity for the rest of your life.

1. Get Your First Cruise Ship Speaking Gig

It all starts here. Once you're ready, you'll need to make contact; either through an agency or with the cruise line directly. Make a compelling presentation and they'll offer you a spot on an upcoming voyage. Don't expect this to happen overnight though.

Occasionally the timing will be just right and they'll be looking to replace someone who dropped out at the last minute. More typically though it can take several months for everything to come together. Once it does, you'll need to have the proper mindset in order to turn this one time speaking gig into a career building opportunity.

Remember, you'll be evaluated after your presentations, so always do your best no matter how many people are in the audience. Be nice to *everybody* while onboard the ship (you never know who's connected to whom).

Also, check in with whomever booked you right after you return from the voyage. They'll already know if your talks went well and you'll want to reiterate that. Give them your availability for upcoming cruises and stay in light but consistent contact until your next booking.

2. Present In Front Of Hundreds Of Prospects
You'll typically present a one hour long talk on each sea day of the cruise. The daily onboard newsletter (called a "patter") will list a blurb about your presentation and give the time and location.

Some speakers get hundreds of people to turn out for their talks while others only get a handful. Occasionally this can be due to the scheduling but mostly it's a result of how you write your blurb and promote your talk.

Write the title and description of your topic so that it evokes curiosity in the reader. So instead of say "Lecture on the Panama Canal: all about the doctor who helped make it possible" you could write something like "Pestilence in Panama: How One Man Discovered

The Cure that Made The Canal Possible". Make your blurb read like the cover of a popular magazine and you'll be on the right track.

In terms of promoting your talk, I've seen some speakers try to chat up the passengers and hand out little cards in advance of their presentations. This strikes me as a very inefficient use of time.

A much better technique is to ask the cruise director if you can be a guest on his morning TV program! This is a show that is broadcast to all the staterooms throughout the entire ship and which most of the passengers watch while they're deciding what to do for the day. If you are invited to do this you should jump at the chance. This will give everyone an opportunity to know who you are and get excited about coming to your presentation. You'll probably only be in a five minute segment of the show, but it can do wonders for your turnout.

You can see a video of one of these morning show segments at my blog here: www.joshuaseth.com/cruise-ship-lecturer-interview

By the way, you won't necessarily be giving all of your talks in the same venue, so make sure you check out the different performance spaces when you first get on board. There is typically a grand theater which seats around a thousand people, a lounge which seats about 500-600, and a dance club which can seat 300-400. Every ship is different though. I've even been on some that have movie theaters that are perfect for delivering enrichment lectures.

Make sure at least one of your lectures is on your primary speaking topic. The people in this particular audience are the best prospects for your list. Most of them won't be in a position to hire you directly, but many of them will work for corporations or organizations that will.

3. Offer BOR Products After Your Talk

BOR or "Back Of the Room" product sales can result in hundreds or even thousands of dollars in revenue after each presentation. Examples of types of products you can sell are CDs, DVDs, and Books. They have to relate to your topic of course and they must look professional in order to be approved by the cruise line. Once they are approved though they are approved forever (just like you) and you can offer them on all your additional cruise ship speaking gigs.

The common thinking among enrichment speakers is that you can only offer these types of products in the gift shop. That is just dead wrong. If you aren't making your Books, CDs, and DVDs immediately available to your audiences directly after your talks you will miss out on the majority of your potential sales. There is a right way and a wrong way in which to do this of course.

A discussion of the finer points of BOR sales is beyond the scope of this book (although it comprises an entire DVD in the Cruise Ship Speaking System). Suffice it to say though that you want to make sure your audience knows what you have available without pushing it so aggressively as to illicit a complaint. One very effective way to do this is by giving away one of your products to an audience participant during your presentation.

I often ask a question of the audience while holding up one of my books or CDs and say that the first person with the correct answer will win a copy. This gets everyone excited to have a copy of my book and reminds them that it's available.

I'm aware that some speakers don't like to "sell" anything at all. This attitude has always mystified me. If what you have to offer will help improve the lives of your audience members then you owe it to them to give them the opportunity to get more of your information. Also, if you're a likable personality then many passengers will want to take a piece of you home with them in the form of one of your products. It's a souvenir and a reminder of the time you've spent together. Why deny them that opportunity?

Do BOR sales right and it can become the most lucrative part of your speaking business.

4. Build Your List For Spin-off Bookings

Whenever you give a presentation of any kind to any sized audience anywhere you should be using that opportunity to build your list. You never know who's in your audience, what they do, who they know, where they work, or how they could help you.

It amazes me how many speakers and entertainers don't bother to do something as simple as passing out a pad of paper to collect names and email addresses. I realize that at certain venues such a tactic would be frowned upon (corporate meetings for instance) but with a little creative thinking much more elegant ways of list building can be employed.

After every talk you should have a way to collect contact information from your audience members. A first name and email is all you need to build a substantial list of prospects in no time.

Remember, people like to buy from those they know, like, and trust. Once they've been a member of your audience you've established that rapport. Don't squander it. Find a way to stay in light contact with them once they're back on land and over time it will result in many more additional bookings and product sales.

The key to effective list building is to give your audience members a reason to hand over their contact information. Simply saying "put down your name to join my list" won't cut it. You have to give them an incentive.

I've personally been able to build a list of well over 10,000 people who have been in my cruise ships audiences and now receive my tip-of-the-week newsletter. In fact, you should sign up for that newsletter yourself so you can see exactly how I do it.

Go to www.7weightlossgifts.com

That is a special website I've set up which offers several free gifts in exchange for your email. I used to just pass a few clipboards around the audience during my lectures and ask people to add their names and emails to the list in exchange for these downloads, but I found that very few of them would ever purchase the upsell items this way.

Whether people buy anything after your talk or not, you want your audience members to sign up for your list. The common advice is to just hand out pads of paper and pens and tell people to put down their name and e-mail if they want to be on your list. The problem with that is that these days people are so inundated with unwanted email that they are unlikely to add their contact information unless you give them some kind of an incentive to do so.

So I developed a give-away, and then a line of give-aways, and put them on a "secret" website. I'd tell my audience that "I have a friends-and-family website where I have a lot of free gifts that I'd like to give you just for being in attendance today."

I began to grow a large list very quickly, which is what everybody wants, right? What I discovered though is that most of those prospects still weren't turning into customers and actually buying anything afterwards. This was because I wasn't asking them to do anything to qualify themselves as prospects, so they didn't really value the give-aways I was providing for them.

Eventually I decided to turn my big list of non-buyers into a smaller list of actual buyers. Now when I introduce the concept of the freebies to my cruise ship audiences I say, "I'd like to give you $97 worth of free gifts after the talk because I only have so much time with you here today and there's a lot more that I'd like to share with you. All you've got to do is come up to the table where the CDs and books are at the back of the room and pick up one of these little "gift cards."

Jet skiing in the Caribbean

They're just postcards, but I never call them that. I call them gift cards because they tell them where to go on the web to claim their free gifts.

And what do we do with postcards? We throw them in the trash, right? Just like business cards, people throw them in the trash. But a gift card people hold onto. Gift cards have intrinsic value. This may seem like a subtle difference, calling postcards gift cards, but it's actually an example of hypnotic language and it can have a powerfully persuasive effect on people.

Two things have now changed in the behavior of the prospect. One, they are making a little bit of an effort to get that card, hold onto it, and put themselves in the database, so what emerges is actually a better list. And two, they have to come to the back of the room table to get their gift cards in the first place.

What happens is it creates a big rush for all the books and CDs as everybody jostles for position in the line. Anybody who was on the fence about buying the products suddenly feels compelled to make a decision. They don't know who's there for the free offer or who's there for the books and CDs. So they all start grabbing everything. They grab all the books. They grab all the CDs. They're thrusting their cards at us as fast as we can handle. I typically need two assistants to help me process all the orders. And now I sell out of everything that I bring on board.

And by the way, the gift shop manager loves this because they share in the revenue you generate. Most cruise lines take a percentage and run everything through the gift shop, so it's in their own best interest that you do well. As long as the products are approved for sale and no one complains about anything, they're happy. They'll even supply you with "shoppies" (girls from the gift shop) to man your BOR table and help process all the orders. It's a good idea to tip them a few bucks for helping out with the rush. You can process a lot more orders that way.

The tip I've just outlined shows you not only how to increase your back of the room product sales it also allows you to make money forever off of your cruise ship talks because you've built a really high quality list in the process. It really doesn't even matter if the cruise line pays you for your talk when you have the opportunity to make that kind of money afterwards.

Now that I employ the special "gift card" strategy described above, I have fewer overall signups to my list but much higher conversion rates from the people who do input their information. In fact, I have an unheard of 30% bounce rate at 7weightlossgifts.com which means that 70% of people who visit that website end up signing up for my list.

Here's a snapshot from my Google Analytics account to prove it.

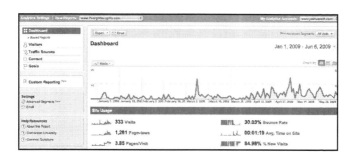

What percentage of people that visit your website end up giving you their contact information? If you're like most speakers, you don't even know.

I have an entire 4 disc training system devoted specifically to showing you how to build your website and automated marketing system over at www.YourWebsiteInAnHour.com Here are the basics of that system:

- Get an unlimited hosting account with www.YourHostWithTheMost.com
- Get an automated shopping cart and list management system with www.YourCartWithTheMost.com
- Use that system to send broadcasts and autoresponders to your list at least monthly
- Offer your products and services to the people on your list along with valuable info
- Keep adding to your prospect and customer list at every appearance you make

- Organically optimize the site for search engines with targeted content that you also share with your list
- Keep developing your relationship with your list and making offers to your list over time so as to extract maximum value from it

Most people think that they have a successful website if it gets a lot of traffic. Guess what? I could care less how much traffic my site gets. What I look for are conversion rates.

If people look around your site and then leave without doing anything then you've gained nothing. What you want them to do is one of two things: either buy or try. Either enquire about booking you for a gig, buy a product, or sign up for your list in exchange for trying out some of your materials for free. And you want those responses in that exact order.

Eventually you will be able determine the total customer value of each person on your list. It might take you a few cruises to get 1,000 people on your list, but they will be valuable prospects: people who already know you and like what you do. Many of them work for or have contacts at organizations that are in a position to hire you.

If you have 1,000 people on your list and only 1% books you for an event in any given year, then you've just generated 10 extra speaking engagements! Even if you only charge $5,000 per event that's an extra $50,000 a year you've just generated simply by following up with the people who were in your audiences on the ships.

If 2% buy your products and your average sale is say $100 then that's an extra $20,000 a year you've just made. That's an extra $70,000 so far and believe me, those percentages are quite conservative.

Have me or someone who knows what they're doing coach you into improving those conversion rates by even just a little bit and you've just created a six figure speaking business!

5. Put On Your Own Seminars At Sea

The real money comes when you start putting on your own events. Let's call this six figure speaking and beyond!

Consider this: you can take that list you've developed and offer them an expanded program relating to your area of expertise. Do this over several days and it's called a seminar. Do it on a cruise ship and it's called a seminar at sea.

What do you know about the people on your list?

- They like to cruise.
- They're interested in your topic area.
- They like you.

It's a simple matter of putting a program together that will appeal to your list and then offering them a "you" cruise. You only need to get a small group together in order for this to be extremely profitable. The minimum number has traditionally been fifteen. As long as you have that many people in your seminar group you'll qualify for discounts on the fares, free tickets, and meeting space onboard the vessel.

You'll generate revenue from the spread between the individual ticket costs and the group discounts you'll be receiving, a split of the broker's commissions for putting the group together, the value of the free tickets (which you can resell to other registrants), the embedded cost of your seminar itself, and any product and coaching sales you make onboard (no need to give a percentage to the cruise line in this case).

It's much easier to get people to register for your events when they're held on a cruise ship as opposed to being in a conference center on land. In many cases your registrants will look at it as a tax deductible vacation (depending on your topic of course). It's also much easier for you to conduct your event as everything is taken care of for you: the meals, the lodging, the entertainment, even the meeting space.

In the next chapter we'll explore just how profitable this final phase in your six figure cruise ship speaking business can be.

The ruins of Pompeii. Just a train ride away from the port in Naples. That's Mt. Vesuvius in the background!

Cruise Ship Speaking On Steroids: Your Own Seminar At Sea

F ar and away the most lucrative form of cruise ship speaking is when you conduct your own seminar. So instead of the cruise line hiring you to speak to their passengers, you provide the passengers and speak only to your own group.

This strategy does take more effort to set up in the first place but the profit potential is huge. You can make money from the cost of each cruise ticket purchased, the speaking fee you bundle into the total cost, the free tickets you will get for approximately every 15 people you bring on board, and the products and services you'll be able to offer your group at the end of your seminar.

Let's say you take a few cruises as an enrichment speaker. You build your list from the people that attend your presentations and stay in contact with them though an automated email followup system (I use www.YourCartWithTheMost.com). Then, when you're ready to put on your own seminar, you already have a list of people who know who you are, have an interest in the subject, and like taking cruises. Success is just a matter of putting everything together and making it happen.

Here's How It Works:

- Come up with a topic you can speak about at length and that people will pay to hear
- Choose a cruise line and itinerary that will appeal to your target market
- Make an offer for a "you" cruise to your list where the cost of the seminar is bundled together with the cost of the cruise.
- Market as necessary to reach your desired number of participants.
- Outline your seminar schedule in such a way that it won't conflict with the port days
- Give great content in your seminar and socialize with your participants at mixers and events on the ship
- Offer them your products and services before the end of the cruise

WHY SEMINARS ON CRUISE SHIPS ARE BETTER THAN SEMINARS ON LAND

It's easier to get people to take a vacation than it is to attend a conference. Because most people will be able to write off these educational cruises, they are essentially taking a tax-free vacation.

Which would you rather do, sit in a cold bare conference room for days on end or take breaks between educational sessions to frolic on an island somewhere? If seminar attendance is a concern for you consider holding your seminar at sea and watch your registrations skyrocket.

People won't miss your sessions. On land, there are many distractions. I know many seminar promoters who prefer to conduct their events in Las Vegas for the same reason I just mentioned. People want to attend educational sessions in fun places, but in Vegas, the strip beckons. There is always a show or a restaurant or casino competing for the attention of your attendees. On a cruise ship, as long as you schedule your sessions on Sea days, you will find your attendance at or near 100%. Everyone can have fun when you are in port and in the evenings, but during the Sea days there is precious little to do other than bake in the sun. That's why the cruise lines hire enrichment lecturers for those days.

It's all inclusive. No wasting time trying to figure out where to go to dinner or how to get from the hotel to the conference center. Everything is all in one place and it's all taken care of for you. This reduces everyone's stress level and helps them to enjoy your event worry free.

You'll get to take a free cruise. Sure, you may get a free hotel room when you put on a land-based seminar, but most cruise lines will give you a free cruise for every 15 passengers you bring on board. Have 60 attendees at your seminar and you've just gotten four free tickets that you can give away, raffle off, or sell to increase your overall profits.

Ever wonder why travel agencies specialize in booking cruises these days? It's because they get big commissions for booking these tickets. The standard commission is 10% of the full price of the cruise. Override commissions kick in for groups. And free tickets are given away for about every 15th ticket within those groups. When you organize your own seminar you will have these profit centers in addition to your registration fees, back of the room sales, and any coaching and consulting work you generate on the back end.

Your group rate can be 20% less than the retail rate an individual would pay to take this same cruise. When you factor in the value of those extra tickets as well as the travel agent commissions (you can probably negotiate a 50/50 split on these with a travel agent since you'll be bringing all the customers and all they'll have to do is book the tickets) your seminar can be in the black before you even set sail.

Let's say you have a general topic like health and wellness or a hobby theme like magic. These kinds of soft topics typically command lower registration fees than hard topics like real estate investing or business development for instance.

Profit oriented seminar topics can command registration fees of several thousand dollars, but let's say you have a topic that's more personal improvement oriented and goes for a lessor fee. Let's say it's music composition and a two day seminar on land would go for $500.

At this point in the process you have a list of 1,000 people who are interested in that topic. You know these people like to cruise. If you offer them a "raw foods cruise" or a "magic at sea" cruise for say $500 more than that cruise would usually cost them, a certain percentage of your list will take you up on the offer.

To keep the math simple, let's say 2% of your list responds to your offer for a theme cruise. That's 20 people. If the cruise normally costs $1,000 then you tack on the $500 for your seminar and all the special activities they'll be invited to as a member of your group (cocktail parties, mixers, dinners and shows together, etc). Right off the bat you're making $10,000 from those 20 registration fees.

But because that fee is bundled into the cost of the cruise ticket you're also making a profit from the group discount you'll get when you book all those tickets at once. This can be as much as 20%. So that's another $2,000. Oh, and don't forget to split the commission with the travel agent. After all, you put the group together, all she has to do is push a button on the computer to purchase the tickets.

Another 10% for your "work" as a travel agent comes to an extra $1,000. Oh, and you can always resell the free ticket you'll get from the cruise line as a result of the size of your group. That's gotta be worth a least another $1,000. Remember, all you've done so far is send an email out to your list. Not too much work for $14,000 profit.

But wait, there's more!

You'll also be able to sell whatever you want at whatever price point you want to the people in your seminar on the ship and keep 100% of the proceeds. It's your group after all. If you have a $1,000 flagship product or a $2,000 coaching program these are the people who would be the most interested in investing in it.

I always like to offer extra bonuses and incentives to my guests at these events which make investing in these programs a no-brainer. And I haven't even touched on what happens when you bring in other people to present to your group or partner with you at these events. You're profits can explode exponentially.

Even in it's simplest form and even with a small group you can make more in 1 seminar at sea than most people make all year.

I conduct a seminar at sea one or twice a year. Get on my professional speaker list at www.CruiseShipSpeaking.com and I'll let you know the next time were setting sail.

How To Get The Gigs: 5 Ways To Get Booked Now

USE AN AGENCY

This is probably the easiest yet least recommended way to get booked speaking on cruise ships. It's the easiest because all you have to do is apply to the agency itself and they will act as the liaison to the cruise line. They have the contacts and know what's available.

An agency's job is to fill these positions for the cruise lines with the appropriate speaker for that voyage. However, this is also the least recommended option because once a speaker's agency connects you with a cruise line then you will always have to go through that agency for any future contracts.

In exchange for the agency making the initial contact on your behalf, you will have to pay them for each and every cruise contract you accept with that line. Yes, pay them. Because enrichment lecturers are unpaid, these agencies are only able to stay in business by charging a fee to their clients (i.e. you). This is fair as they are performing a service for you.

The question you must ask yourself is whether this is a service you could just as well perform yourself. Instead of calling an agency, are you capable of calling the cruise line directly? Instead of submitting your materials to the agency, do you feel comfortable submitting them to the cruise line itself? Is so, then you can probably skip this option and save yourself from having to pay a middleman in perpetuity.

One exception though: guest entertainers can be well served by having the right agent. Guest entertainers, unlike enrichment lecturers, do get paid for their contracts. These payments are usually in the range of several thousand dollars a week. An entertainment agency will get a cut of that (called a commission) ranging from 10-20%. As long as it's a good agency this can be well worth it, as entertainment contracts are a lot more complicated than enrichment lecturer contracts.

So what makes for a good agent?

Well, first of all a good agent must actually have contacts at the cruise lines that can help you to get booked. If they don't have a preexisting relationship then you may as well just form one yourself.

Beyond that, a good agent must do more than simply match people to contracts. They must be advocates and not just order takers. The entertainers I know who don't use agents for their cruise ship work refuse to do so for precisely this reason. They maintain that the agents are simply order takers and don't do anything they couldn't accomplish themselves. While that may be true some of the time (or possibly most of the time) it doesn't have to be that way.

I personally have different agents representing me in different markets, including the cruise ship market. I am on a first name basis with all of my agents and maintain a personal relationship with most of them. Two of my agents even came to my wedding!

To be sure, that is not the typical agent / client relationship. You must work to create that kind of a bond. It doesn't automatically appear once you become a client. But once you do create this kind of a bond then your agents can and will go out of their way to help you. They'll help to smooth out booking conflicts, travel emergencies, and touchy subjects (like raises).

I recently turned down quite a few contracts from a particular cruise line because they wanted me to perform twice as many shows for the same pay. This was inequitable and I refused to accept it. If I had turned down those contracts myself it may have cost me my relationship with the cruise line. Because I had an agency acting as an intermediary though, they were able to renegotiate the terms, reduce the number of required shows, and increase the pay. Thank you agents :-)

So the bottom line is: if you're strictly a speaker, go ahead and contact the cruise lines directly, but make sure you're fully prepared before you do. Don't risk burning your bridges. I recommend going through the complete Cruise Ship Speaking System described at the end of this book before you make contact. A little preparation goes a long way in this business and it can pay off big time.

If you're an entertainer who's reading this book because you want to add speaking and product sales to your offerings than whether to use an agent or not becomes more of a personal preference.

If you already book all of your own gigs in other markets then you may as well continue that approach with the cruise lines. They're just big corporations after all. And just like booking a corporate gig, there's always a person or a small committee that's going to make the final decision to hire you. It's just a matter of putting the right materials in front of the right people at the right time.

Personally, I like to outsource everything except my shows, seminars, coaching, and product creation. Everything else I hand off to other people. This seems like the highest and best use of my time. If you're not there yet (or if you like doing everything yourself) then go ahead and book direct. Just make sure you're fully prepared before you do.

TAKE A CRUISE

Want to short cut the process and get in front of the decision makers right away? Then simply book yourself on a cruise with the line for whom you'd like to work and arrange to give a lecture on the voyage.

You'll have to pay for the cruise of course, but once you book the passage it's a simple matter to contact the entertainment department, explain that you're a passenger on this particular cruise, and ask to present a lecture onboard in consideration for becoming an enrichment lecturer in the future.

If you present yourself well, with appropriately titled lecture topics and "credentials" then there's really no reason for them to say no to your request. Cruise lines like to treat their passengers very well and the only hesitation they might have is if they think you won't be capable of pulling it off. If you do a bad job it will reflect poorly on the cruise line. So again, make sure you have all your ducks in a row before you make contact so as to instill confidence and certainty.

Introduce yourself to the cruise director while onboard and ask for one of his staff to review your presentation. Don't make a pest of yourself but explain that you'd like to be considered for a position as an enrichment lecturer on future voyages and you're using this presentation as a sort of audition so they can assess the quality of your work.

Now all you have to do is deliver a solid presentation and use the review as a springboard to future bookings!

SUBMIT DIRECTLY TO THE CRUISE LINE

Every cruise line has an entertainment department which is responsible for booking the entertainers and guest lecturers. They get many requests each and every day from people just like you who want to do this kind of work.

What separates the professionals from the dilettantes is the quality of the materials. If you submit a homemade DVD with your name written in sharpie on the face of it, it will most likely get filed in the circular bin. If on the other hand you have sharp, well organized, high quality presentational materials along with intriguing lecture topics and relevant credentials they will go a long way toward instilling the confidence necessary for you to get hired.

Presentational materials you'll want to include are:

- Your headshot
- Your bio
- Your resume (relevant to your lecture topics)
- Your references (list of places where you've spoken before)
- Your proposed lecture topics (with alternate choices)

- Your demo tape (10 minutes or less)
- Optional: Your book (this can help you get any kind of speaking engagement)

ADD IT TO YOUR ENTERTAINMENT SERVICES

If you already perform on cruise ships and you're reading this book to expand your services, then simply adding a lecture to one of the sea days that take place after your show is as simple as coming up with a topic and a product. All you need is to have something to say and something to sell and you're in business.

Hypnotists can conduct seminars on self-hypnosis, magicians can conduct magic classes, jugglers can teach juggling, I've even worked with a hula hoop performer who is now developing an exercise DVD and class based on hula-hooping.

One of the highest grossing entertainers I've seen on ships is a comedian who does a lecture on finding the humor in illness and dying. It's a delicate subject that he handles expertly and entertainingly. His lecture packs the room and he sells out of his books and BOR products afterwards with regularity.

If you're an entertainer who's not yet booked to perform on ships, then add one of these types of presentations to your promo packet and it will make you a more desirable act for the cruise lines to book in the first place. You can "fill more slots" as they say. Present it right and it almost seems like they're getting an extra show for free (while you're increasing your revenue through the product sales).

GATHER YOUR OWN GROUP AND BOOK YOURSELF

By far the most lucrative form of cruise ship speaking is to your own group. Review the previous chapter for a discussion of how to do this.

Remember, no one needs to give you permission to speak on cruise ships. You can simply do it. You can book yourself on a cruise and make it happen directly. You can put together your own group and leapfrog all the other steps.

It takes guts. Most people won't do it. But I want to impress upon you that you can. If you already have your own customer list then why not tap into their collective buying power and just put on your own seminar at sea?

Email me at info@joshuaseth.com if you need help with this endeavor. It can be incredibly profitable, productive, and fun. And it's easier than you think when you know how!

In Rio De Janeiro, Brazil

Turning Free Into Fee: Types Of BOR Sales You Can Do

A fter every talk (or show) you do you should make products available to your audience members. Some speakers and entertainers don't like the idea of selling though and deny their audience members this opportunity. This kind of thinking is completely backwards and does a disservice to your audience members and yourself.

There is only so much content you can deliver in an hour. If your audience wants more of what you have to say then why not give it to them? Even if it's the same content you just delivered but in recorded form, why not give your audience members a chance to relive the experience or share it with their friends?

The fact is, you owe it to your audience members to give them the opportunity to extend the experience you've shared together through your books, CDs, and DVDs.

Let's go over each of these three forms of BOR products: why you should offer them, how you can price them, and the basics of how to create them as well.

A CD RELATED TO YOUR TALK

The simplest BOR product you can create is a CD. It's also the product that commands the least value. Still, you can sell hundreds of CDs on a single cruise so it does add up.

The gift shop will determine the price at which you sell your CDs. Typically $16 or $20. Some cruise lines (such as NCL at the moment) don't require set prices for different types of BOR products. This is the exception though and not the rule.

Most cruise lines will require that you get your products approved before selling them on their ships. This is primarily to insure that they are professionally packaged and produced.

If you have never created your own spoken word CD before you'll be surprised at just how simple the process has become. In it's most basic form, your CD can simply be a recording of the talk you'll be giving on the ship.

Why would people buy a recording of the same talk they just heard? Well some people won't be able to make the entire presentation and will get it to listen to later. Some people will just want it as a souvenir of the cruise to share with their friends back home. And some people will like you so much that they'll want to have something with your picture on it so you can sign it for them.

I'm not joking. You'll be like a mini-celebrity on the cruise and people will want to take their pictures with you and get your autograph. Make it easy for them by putting your picture on at least some of your products and always carrying a sharpie pen for autographs.

If you want to edit the content of your CD recording then use one of the following free programs:

- Mac: Use the free Garage Band application that came with your iLife software.
- Windows: Download the free Audacity software off the web. It's flexible and easy to use.

TIP: Make sure to mention your website at the beginning and end of your recording. The best way to get the listener to actually visit your website is to offer them something of value that relates to the recording. Tell them that they can get "x" for free at your site as a bonus for investing in your product. That's what my www.7weightlossgifts.com site is for. I only give it out to people in my weight loss seminars on the ships. This way I get them on my list whether they buy anything immediately or not. You should do the same thing.

A PACKAGE OF CDS RELATED TO YOUR TALK

Who says you have to sell only one CD title or only sell them one at a time? Everybody loves package deals and they result in bigger sales overall (even if you give bonus CDs away in the package).

I've tested all sorts of combinations, from individual CD sales, to 2 for 1 deals, to buy 2 get 1 free offers, to 6 CD systems. The combination that works best for you will depend on what your topic is and how you pitch it. I do suggest testing different offers though and keeping close track of the results.

If you create a set of 6 CDs, as I have done with my weight loss hypnosis system (available at www.WeightLossHypnosisSystem.com), then it only takes 10 people to generate a thousand dollars worth of sales. It's a lot easier to motivate 10 people to buy something than it is to motivate 60 people to buy something, even if the price points are different.

Create various package offers, test them out, analyze the results, and implement the ones that are the most profitable. It'll make a big difference in your bottom line.

Currently, as a result of this kind of experimentation, I am *not* offering my weight loss hypnosis book for sale on the ships. I only offer it as a signed bonus to people who invest in the complete 6 CD system. This has boosted the sales of these six packs so much that giving the book away has become a great investment for me and a prized reward for them.

Think creatively about what kinds of BOR packages you can offer and what kinds of bonuses you can add to them to increase their desirability. This can be a very fun game to play and quite profitable as well!

A DVD OR MULTI DVD SET

The gift shops onboard the cruise ships price DVDs at a premium to CDs. Typically they're set at $25. Many speakers and entertainers simply set up a camera in the back of the room during one of their presentations, record it, and create a DVD out of the content.

If you have a Mac, you can edit the footage together using iMovie and burn it to a DVD in iDVD. This is what I use myself, even though I own higher end software. iMovie is really all you need.

If you have a Windows computer, you can use Sony Vegas Movie Studio which can be purchased for as little as $50 from www.sonycreativesoftware.com

Another way to create a DVD is to record a voiceover while doing a screen capture of your PowerPoint presentation. This sounds like it would be dry and mind-numbing, but I've actually seen some very engaging products created this way. If you have a Mac then you can use the Keynote software that comes with iWork to create this type of Powerpoint presentation.

For screen capture, the industry standard is Camtasia, which is available for both Mac and Windows at www.techsmith.com

Once you've finished your DVD and burned your master disc, you'll have to get it duplicated. I use DiscMakers for large runs. I've found their prices, quality, customer service, and turnaround times to be excellent. Plus, they can even ship your order directly to the port agent who will have them waiting for you when you board the ship!

You can find DiscMakers online at www.discmakers.com/

YOUR OWN BOOK
(BEST FOR CREDIBILITY AND SPIN-OFF BUSINESS)

While writing your own book is definitely the most time consuming BOR product on this list it is also the most beneficial.

Authors are held in high esteem in our society and once you write your own book on your area of expertise you will benefit from that perception.

You will be considered an expert in your field and that can translate to publicity opportunities, speaking engagements, increased attendance, and greater sales of all your other products and services.

Writing your own book is something that every speaker should do. In fact, it's so important that I've devoted the entire next chapter to breaking down the process and showing you how to do it.

Ahhh, Rome. A frequent stop on
European cruises.

How Writing A Book Can Help Your Speaking Business

Have you ever thought about taking your speaking business to the next level by writing your own book?

It's not as hard as you think and it can yield dividends for the rest of your life.

Being the person who literally wrote the book on your area of expertise can be a great way to establish authority and get gigs. Why work to convince someone that you're the expert in your field when your book can do that for you?

People don't even need to read the book. Simply by having your name on the cover and your picture on the back you've gained so much credibility that they're now open to hearing what you have to say.

Writing your own book will give you instant credibility in your field, opportunities for publicity in your business, and a way to presell your customers with educational content that will lead them back to you as the person they know, like, and trust to solve the problems you address.

And your book can open up whole new speaking opportunities for you as well. Whole new revenue streams. Let me rip back the curtain and show you how writing a book can quickly and easily take your speaking business to a whole new level.

YOUR BOOK IS THE MAGIC TICKET

As a speaker, you should seek to leverage your time by communicating your message to as many people at once as possible. Sure, you could take out advertising but that's expensive. What if there was a way to get exposed to new markets, land additional gigs, and get massive media exposure without paying anything at all. Now there's an idea!

There is a way to get all the free publicity you want for your business and I'll bet you've already figured out what that is. That's right, the absolute best way I know to get free publicity, credibility, and new business is by writing a book in your area of expertise.

This has been my experience personally. My book "The Weight Loss Hypnosis Solution" is a natural outgrowth of my speaking business and the product of information I already knew.

Because of my book, I have a steady stream of new prospects plus I no longer have to "sell" my hypnosis CDs directly. I can provide an inexpensive solution to people's problems through my book and they can choose to complete the system with the hypnosis CDs on their own. This two step process allows prospects to enter my sales funnel through an impulse buy (the $20 book) and then flow through to the somewhat larger investment in the CDs. The book creates a level of credibility that the CDs alone cannot provide. It also becomes an important educational tool for the consumer and keeps me from having to repeat the same information over and over again.

I also give away the first 40 pages of the book (along with a lot of other goodies) at my lead generation site. This "try before you buy" approach makes it easy to establish a relationship with people. There is no risk, no cost, and no obligation for the consumer. Before they know it they are learning from me, benefiting from my advice, and wanting more. This is how you turn short-term prospects into long-term customers.

After my seminar the other day, a man came up to shake my hand and congratulate me on the presentation. He introduced himself as a motivational speaker.

Great, I thought, I wonder if that's a copy of his book he's holding in his hands? It wasn't. Turns out he's "working on it." I instantly knew he's not really a motivational speaker, he just wants to be one someday. His credibility was shot, just like that.

It's a shame too, because as difficult as it is to write a book the traditional way, the "Your Book In A Month" methods I teach make the whole process really fun and efficient.

I just went though this process with one of my coaching clients and although it did take him 31 days he now has his own book and has already gotten two speaking engagements out of it.

He's a motivational speaker too. The only difference is he has a book and is actually being paid to speak!

What about in your own speaking business? Imagine how having your own book will help you leapfrog your competition, educate your customers, and gain publicity opportunities paid advertising just can't buy.

I used to have a hard time getting 30 people to show up for my weight loss hypnosis seminars. Now that I literally "wrote the book on the subject" I regularly get over 300 people coming to hear me talk about the exact same thing!

Having a self-published book has changed my business and my life. It will change yours too.

Having your own book on your field of expertise will:
- Brand you as an expert in your field
- Give you a competitive advantage
- Create massive credibility and prestige
- Give you lots of publicity opportunities
- And open up whole new revenue streams

I think the main reason speakers don't get their book done is it just seems like too big a project. It seems overwhelming. And in truth, if you go the traditional publishing route it certainly can be.

You have to put the whole manuscript together yourself (which can take some people years), prepare a proposal and chase down an agent. If you're lucky enough to get one then you have to start courting publishers. And if you manage to jump that hurdle you still have to wait about a year before going to press.

Yeah, that old way of getting your book published was a lot of work and typically for very little payoff.

Compare that to self publishing, where you can have your book printed on demand for a few bucks a copy and have it in your hands in a few days. It's dead simple now... oh, except for that actual "writing" part.

What if I told you there was a way to get your book done without actually writing anything?

Shhhh... there is.

I'm not talking about ghostwriters either. These will be your own ideas put down in print.

I'm also not talking about using one of those "vanity presses" that charge you an arm and a leg.

Who needs 'em! Not us. Not now...

YOU CAN WRITE AND SELF PUBLISH YOUR BOOK IN A MONTH

Sometimes you just need a little push to get started. That's what I've found with my coaching clients in the "Your Book In A Month" program. Every single one of them had wanted to write a book for years but never knew how to get started. Now that they have, they're flying through the process with relative ease.

Sure, there have been some hiccups. That's natural whenever you push yourself beyond your comfort zone and create something new. But

Cruise Ship Speaking Joshua Seth

it's also exciting to get that book out of your head and onto the page!

With all the news about rising unemployment figures, massive layoffs, and prolonged recession, my coaching clients are living a different reality. By writing their own books they are creating a lead generation tool for their speaking businesses, a source of new revenue, a vehicle that can generate free publicity, and more.

They are creating opportunities and so can you.

WHAT TO WRITE ABOUT

That's easy. Just be outcome oriented. What action do you want the reader to take as a result of being exposed to your book? Work backwards from there.

I wanted people to see me as an expert in my field and not just an entertainer. I had this idea to start running weight loss hypnosis seminars the day after my shows but hardly anybody came. They thought of me as a performer and that did not translate to seminar attendance.

It was only when I literally wrote the book on my subject that I found it easy to fill seminar seats and establish myself as an expert in the field.

Now I close my cruise ship shows by holding up my book and talking about how hypnosis can be used for more than just fun and games, it's actually a great way to lose weight. And I tell them about my seminar. If I don't have a seminar scheduled, the book itself upsells them to my 6 CD self hypnosis set on the topic. If they don't get the book they can still get all the downloadable freebies on my squeeze-page and fall into my sales funnel that way. Everybody wins, but without the book to establish credibility in the first place none of this would ever happen.

FOLLOW THIS SIMPLE 7 STEP FORMULA WHEN OUTLINING YOUR BOOK

1. Define your reader's problem in their own words

2. Agitate the ways in which not solving this problem immediately can hurt them (turn up the pain in order to motivate them to take solution oriented action)

3. List all the things to beware of when they're looking for a solution (disqualifying your competitors in the process)

4. List the ways in which you've been able to provide those solutions in your business (which gives you an opportunity to provide social proof)

5. Destroy the myths and misconceptions that people have about your product or service (subtly answering their objections in the process)

6. Offer them an incentive to let you help them solve that problem and build in a strong call to action (your offer)

7. Show how you have already helped other people just like them by including lots of testimonials throughout

I'll bet you could sit down and outline your book right now couldn't you?

Of course, you'll have to refine and shape that outline into something suitable for your book and your topic, but the basic formula should be clear to you just from reading the 7 steps listed above.

How To Write It Quickly

You don't need to spend months or years writing your book. This isn't going to be the great American novel after all. In the interest of full disclosure, I should mention here that it did take me eight months to write my first book and nearly that many rewrites. The problem was that I started the process by having one of my seminars transcribed and then filling things in from there.

What I should have done is start with an outline! Having an outline cuts down on the work (and the rewrites) enormously. The book you now hold in your hands was written in 6 days and edited in 4. I documented the entire process at www.joshuaseth.com/write-your-book

One of the ways I've been able to help my coaching clients shortcut the process to write and self publish their own books within a month is is to create a strong outline first. Then we record a phone interview where I ask them questions stemming from their outline and follow up on their answers with more questions that create even more content. We then send the mp3 of that interview to a transcription service and their answers become the rough draft of the book. No writing is necessary

From there it's an easy matter of outsourcing the editing, layout, and design work through elance or a similar service. Now that your book is done you'll need to answer that controversial question...

Should You Self Publish Or Try To Get A Traditional Publisher

The choice of whether to self publish or go through the traditional publishing process will depend on your goals. In general though, while there is certainly still more prestige associated with traditional publishing and a chance for wider distribution, I suggest that you self publish at least your first book. It will short cut the process and provide many benefits right away.

Get it out there. Get it done. Start helping people and building your business with it right away. Use your book for positioning and lead generation as soon as you can. It's the best kind of business card you can have but it's utterly ineffective if it just sits there on your hard drive gathering nano-dust.

Don't let yourself get paralysis by analysis, just get the thing done and get it out there. You can always sell it to a publishing house later if you want to.

HERE ARE 3 THINGS TO AVOID WHEN SELF PUBLISHING YOUR BUSINESS BUILDING BOOK:

1. Don't Use A Vanity House. If you find yourself getting enticed by an offer to do everything for you in exchange for some five figure fee, splash a glass of cold water in your face and wake up. This process isn't difficult, you just need to know where to get certain things done (such as which printing house Amazon uses so you don't have to mess around with fulfilling orders yourself).

2. Don't Make Your Book Too Big. No one will read it. Better to be brief and leave them wanting more than to intimidate them with your towering tome. Also, it's cheaper to print and ship your book if it's a little over 100 pages than if it's twice that size.

3. Don't Let Anyone Else Own the ISBN Number. Whoever owns the ISBN number owns your book. Make sure that person is you.

Cruise Ship Speaking Joshua Seth

Your Next Step

I've created a series of training videos designed to help speakers and entrepreneurs who want all the benefits of having their own book with the minimum investment of time, trouble, and expense. Check it out at www.YourBookInAMonth.com

3 Things You Must Not Do Or Risk Walking The Plank

A s with any professional speaking market, there are certain "unwritten rules" you must be aware of in order to keep your booking. For instance, if you've ever spoken in the corporate market, you'll know how important it is to keep your presentation to the exact time you've agreed upon with the client.

The cruise market has several such unwritten rules which, if you break them, can result in your termination. Some should be obvious (like missing the ship). Others, less so. All of them are important for you to be aware of so you don't end up walking the plank in the middle of your contract!

Here's a list of the top 3 things you never want to do on a cruise ship (they could cost you your job):

Never Be Rude To Anyone
Or Complain About Anyone (onstage or off)

Passengers review you at the end of the cruise, not the end of your presentation, so even if you do a great job on stage they can still rate you poorly if you cut in front of them in the buffet line.

You are representing the cruise line the entire time you're on board, so consider that you're onstage from the moment you embark to the moment you disembark and put on a happy face.

Think of a cruise ship as you would a floating summer camp. After a while everybody knows what everyone else is up to and they love gossiping about it. If you talk about people behind their back it will travel all around the ship until that person is staring you in the face. Don't do it. You never know who's connected to whom.

So be really nice to everybody and easy to work with. This is not the place to be a prima donna. It's the place to be a team player. You do that and it's going to help you get a lot of cruise ship gigs over the long term.

Never Get Drunk In The Public Areas

There once was a very affable crooner who would play piano and sing songs all night in one of the lounges of a ship I've worked on often. At the time I would fly down to meet this ship in the Caribbean every other week and would always be greeted by this fellow's smiling face as his cabin was only two doors down from mine.

One day I boarded the ship and he was gone. I knew his contract was supposed to run for several more months so I asked about him.

Everyone was extremely eager to tell me exactly what happened and how he had gotten himself kicked off the ship (see #1 above).

Turns out he liked to go to the disco up on the 18th floor of the ship after he finished his own musical numbers for the night. There he'd while away the wee hours of the morning dancing and drinking with the pretty girls until he was able to entice one of them into more intimate activities.

Sleeping with the passengers almost made this list. It is frowned upon, but apparently it's not enough to get you kicked off the ship as this behavior went on for quite some time. One night though he excused himself to visit the lavatory as he'd had quite a bit to drink... and he never came back.

Eventually the disco closed, the girls all went back to their cabins, and our friend was nowhere to be found. Enter the cleaning crew. Sloshing their buckets and seeking entry into the men's room they found it to be locked tight against them. As they were unable to gain entry they had no choice but to call security.

Security had to force the door open as there was a heavy weight pressed up against it. Can you guess what it was? Right, it was our musical friend, passed out, with his pants around his ankles and reeking of last night's booze. He was put off the ship at the next port.

The moral of our story: don't get drunk in the public areas.

... get drunk in the crew bar instead ;-)

NEVER MISS THE SHIP!

This does happen from time to time and it's expensive. You have to arrange lodgings for the night and purchase transportation to meet the ship in the next port the following day (which can often be in another country). It's also grounds for dismissal.

While they won't necessarily terminate your contract for missing the ship, they can. Oftentimes when the ship is about to leave port and sailors are ready to pull up the gangway there will be a series of announcements over the loudspeaker asking Mr. and Mrs. such and such to come to the passenger services desk. These are people that are going to miss the ship.

The crew makes these announcements to see if those missing passengers are somehow onboard, but they never are. They're usually in a taxi somewhere, racing for the pier, having forgotten about the difference between ships' time and local time.

The ship always leaves on "ship's time". Whatever time it is on shore is of no relevance to the time the ship is leaving. Make sure you are aware of the difference whenever you leave the ship so it'll still be there when you return.

I'll close this section out with another story: not too long ago I was on a ship with a very funny ventriloquist. He had invited his parents to join him on this particular cruise and they were all looking forward to spending some time together at sea.

His parents were excited to see their son perform in the big theater on this particular night as it was the only night of the cruise when he would be doing his full show. It was an island day, but his parents went back on board early to get ready for the evening's performance.

Our hero, the ventriloquist, lingered in the internet cafe on the pier checking emails. He could see the ship just outside from his window as he typed blissfully away, secure in the knowledge that he had until 5:00pm until that whistle blowed.

"Bwah-Bwah!" The ship's horn pierced the air, blowing him out of his seat and running down the pier, as it left the port a full hour early. Or did it? It left on "ship's time" and left our ventriloquist behind.

His parent's were back onboard of course, seriously considering adopting the dummy :-)

Shoreside view of a departing cruise ship

Cruise Ship Speaking Joshua Seth

Stories From The 7 Seas: Thailand

S uzy and I arrived in Thailand not knowing where we would go
or where we would stay and proceeded to have a day filled with
uniquely adventurous experiences.

When we disembarked the ship I went straight to the taxi line, looking
for a group that I could split a fare with. Several people were hiring a
van to go to the beach town Pattaya and for $15 Suzy and I joined
them.

We got off at the first stop with a couple who was staying at a
beachfront resort and attempted to haggle with the front desk for a
room. They wouldn't budge on their inflated walk-up price, so I went
over to the internet center in the lobby and booked the room for 1/2
price on the internet. Minutes later we had a beautiful room in the 4
star resort for $45. Still expensive for Thailand, but it's a resort at the
beach in the high season after all.

We dropped off our stuff and walked down to the beach. Beautiful
and exotic, but nothing new for us, so we jumped on the back of
motorcycles and sped into town.

Pattaya itself is a seedy affair, somewhat reminiscent of the beaches at Rio but with a thick veneer of sleaze left over from the GIs in WWII. Middle aged westerners getting massages on the beach and walking around hand in hand with petite young Thai girls. That sort of thing.

We ducked into an upscale mall across the street and Suzy was in heaven. Shop after shop of the most exquisitely exotic silks and sculptures and paintings and outfits and on and on and on. I've never seen anything like it myself. And all very cheap too. Still, we're waiting to do our shopping in Bangkok, so we left and had lunch at a well reviewed high-end Thai restaurant where we sipped blended juices from pineapples, sampled various local cuisines, and tried in vain to smother the fire on our tongues with heapings of fried rice. Total cost for lunch for two in a private room filled with traditional music and overlooking tropical vistas... $15.

Next up... trekking through the jungle on elephants! We rode quite a ways out of town to get to the elephant conservatory and had one of the best excursions I've ever been on. We rode elephants through rivers and jungles, played with wild monkeys, floated along on a bamboo raft while throwing pellets into the water that attracted hundreds of giant fish, rode on ox drawn carts to a clearing in the woods where we feasted on Thai food and watched traditional Thai dancers, sword fighters, and fire jugglers. Six hours later we emerged, exhausted but thrilled with our day so far.

Riding elephants in Thailand

Time to head back to the resort for some Royal Thai massages! Suzy and I both agree they were by far the best we'd ever had. A full hour each, intensive and in a spa like setting, and for only $6 each. By this time we were ready for bed, but couldn't end our day in Pattaya without visiting the infamous Walking Street, the stuff of traveler's legends.

At the Golden Palace in Bangkok, Thailand

I didn't bring a camera and we carried our money in our shoes because I thought for sure we'd be pick-pocketed, but it all felt surprisingly safe. That said, it was unlike anything I've ever seen and beyond what I'm prepared to describe in detail. Let's just say it's a pulsing mass of humanity, sweating in the sultry midnight heat, with hundreds of girls dancing and flirting and performing in the clubs and on the street. Picture Blade Runner but a thousand times more intense. We got back to the resort sometime before daybreak and collapsed on the bed instantly.

As I write this the following morning we're in the back of a private car I hired to take us in air conditioned comfort to our 4.5 star hotel right in the middle of the action in Bangkok. It's a 2 hr drive and I didn't want to mess around with shared transport. I know I'm being ripped off for the fare, but who cares. It's still only $40.

We've got 5 days and 4 nights to explore Bangkok before we fly to Trinidad via London to join yet another Caribbean cruise. On this

Firedancing show in Thailand

month's tour we will have flown entirely around the world and then some and visited for anywhere from a few hours to a few days Japan, Singapore, Vietnam, Cambodia, Thailand, London, Trinidad, St. Lucia, Dominican Republic, and St. Barts. What did Jackie Mason used to say... "It's a living"!

Frequently Asked Questions

How much demand is there for cruise ship speakers?

Look at it this way. There are lots and lots of cruise lines out there. But let's just say Princess, for instance, because I've done a lot of work with them. They have 18 ships on their line. Each one of those ships goes out 52 weeks a year. 18x52= 936. So that's almost a thousand cruises a year. Sometimes they even have two enrichment lecturers on each ship. So there's well over a thousand speaking opportunities just on Princess each and every year.

Then multiply those results by all the other lines out there: Disney and Cunard and Carnival and NCL and Royal Caribbean and so on. Even if they only have one port lecturer, there are still thousands and thousands of opportunities for you to get booked on cruise ships.

Is it hard to get these gigs?

Yes and no. It can be very easy once you know exactly how to do it. Then again, it can be a frustrating experience if you just blindly pick up the phone and take a shot in the dark.

Cruise Ship Speaking   Joshua Seth

There are basically two ways to get booked to speak on cruise ships. One is to contact the cruise line directly. And two is to use an agency. I suggest contacting the cruise lines directly. If you use an agency to get booked as an enrichment lecturer, you will be locked in to using them for that cruise line from that point forward. Since they require a fee for their services, it's much better to make contact with the cruise line directly whenever possible.

Later in this guide book I've given you a listing of all the major cruise lines that are likely to hire you as a speaker. I've included toll-free telephone numbers whenever possible as well as websites. Use those web links to do research into the cruise lines before you contact them. Get a sense of what kind of passengers they cater to and the different itineraries they offer. This information can be invaluable to you when preparing your lecture topics and press kits.

With the right research, preparation, and presentation getting these gigs can indeed be easy.

How many talks will I need to give?

Typically you will only need to give your talks on sea days. When the ship is in port the passengers disembark the vessel in order to go sightseeing. On a seven-day cruise there may only be two sea days. Occasionally the ship may miss a port because of weather and in that case it's a good idea to have an extra talk prepared.

It's much better to be overprepared than overwhelmed. Of course every voyage is different, but three talks in total during a seven-day sailing is a good benchmark.

Have an extra lecture topic in mind in case you miss a port and make sure at least one of your lectures relates to your primary area of expertise so you can use it to develop a targeted list and build your speaking business back on land.

How long does each talk need to be?

The schedule will be set by the cruise director and you only know this once you are on board the vessel. It's almost always one hour per talk though. Occasionally they will want you to only go for 45 or 50 minutes. Usually this is because they want to give the passengers time to make it to the next event. If the next event is revenue-generating for the cruise line than that takes precedence over your talk.

TIP: It's better to leave information out of your talk then to go over time. Never go over time. There are a lot of activities planned throughout the day and if your presentation throws off the schedule they will not like it. Also, be particularly aware of when Bingo and the art auctions are scheduled. These are big revenue-generating activities for the cruise lines and you want to make sure not to interfere with them.

How many people are in the typical audience?

Brace yourself... anywhere from 10 to 1,000. Seriously. If you choose your talk well, have an eye-catching title, and present in the theater, it is possible to fill every seat in the house. Let me tell you, you can sell a lot of books and CDs after your talk when there are 1000 people in attendance.

On the other hand, it is possible to be scheduled at an inconvenient time in an unfamiliar room with an unpopular topic and only have a dozen or so people show up.

Cruise Ship Speaking   Joshua Seth

The good news is that you do have a lot of control over which of these scenarios occurs. The key is to choose your topic well relevant to your target audience on that particular voyage. Although you don't need to change your talk for every cruise it is a good idea to know whether you will be talking to college kids or senior citizens.

Depending on the time of year, the size and age of the vessel, and which cruise line it is, the exact same itinerary can attract very different sets of passengers. Generally speaking, the longer the voyage the more expensive it will be and therefore the older the passenger it will attract.

On the other hand, 3-4 day cruises to the Caribbean are invariably stuffed full of party hearty twenty-somethings. My suggestion is to seek out the cruise lines and the voyages that you would personally enjoy taking. That way you'll be combining business with pleasure and having the best of both worlds.

Who pays for the travel?

If you're a guest entertainer as I am then the cruise line will pay for your travel. If you're strictly a speaker then you will be expected to pay for your own travel to and from the ship. If that is the case, you may want to initially apply to speak for cruises that leave from ports close to home.

Can I access my email at sea?

Yes, you can access the Internet just as you would at home. There is a computer center provided to the passengers as well as wireless areas of the ship that are available 24/7. Of course you won't want to use that because the rates the passengers pay are ridiculously high. An entire DVD in the complete Cruise Ship Speaking System is devoted to showing you how to get deeply discounted rates on services all over the ship, including Internet and satellite phone calls.

Can I make calls while at sea?

Yes, you can usually make calls right from the phone in your room, even when you're in the middle of the ocean. When you use the crew calling card (that l show you how to get in the DVD I mentioned above) it will only cost you a few cents a minute and you can avoid the huge international roaming charges that passengers pay when using their cell phones at sea. Having a highly profitable speaking business means both saving money as well as earning it after all.

Can I take a traveling companion?

You can share your cabin with anyone you like: a spouse, a friend, a relative, or even an enemy if you're really into that whole " keep your friends close but keep your enemies closer" thing :-)

Riding scooters in Cozumel, Mexico

Here's a great idea: you can offer a free cruise to your friend in exchange for the airfare. That's a win-win for both of you since a plane ticket costs a lot less than a cruise!

What kind of a cabin will I get?

This will vary according to the cruise line and the vessel that you're on. For instance, I have found that within a single cruise line I have boarded different ships and gotten an officer's cabin on one and a passenger cabin on another. Don't worry though, you won't get a below decks crew cabin.

Most lines will give you full passenger status so you'll be put in a passenger cabin. It may be an inside cabin without a view though. Either that or an officer's cabin. An officer's cabin does have a view but it's sometimes through a porthole rather than a full window.

But really, who cares about the view from the cabin? If it's too much trouble to get out of bed and walk up on deck to take a look around, you can always turn on the front of the ship channel. This thrilling television offering features a static camera shot of whatever's in front of the ship. Just leave that station on and look at that instead of the window. Bam, instant view!

What if I get seasick?

I can honestly say that in over 100 cruises I have never gotten seasick. There have been a couple of days where we had really choppy seas though. Both times were coming from or going to Bermuda. Bermuda is stuck way out there in the middle of the Atlantic Ocean and can see some pretty rough weather. Still, today's huge ocean liners have stabilizers that keep the ships remarkably steady.

If you are at all concerned about this, you can always have your doctor prescribe one of those patches that goes behind your ear. It's called a Transderm Scopolamine Patch. You'll see passengers wearing this all over the ship (even when they are in port)!

If you prefer to go the non-medicated route, you can also get elastic wristbands called "Sea bands" that press down on an acupressure point about 3 inches from your wrist. These work amazingly well for a lot of people. If you're not one of them, there's always Dramamine.

These last two options are usually available in the gift shop on board the cruise ship. They will sell out quickly however, so if you want them either get them before you come on board or immediately after sailing.

High above the still waters of the Mediterranean
on Santorini, Greece

Talk the Talk: Glossary of Nautical Terminology

You will be expected to talk the talk when you step aboard a luxury ocean liner for your first gig as a cruise ship speaker. If you're not familiar with the terminology this can be quite confusing. I didn't know the difference between fore and aft or bow and stern for the longest time. Here's a handy glossary of words you'll hear on board a cruise ship and rarely anywhere else.

Aft: the back or rear of the ship. Literally means "after amidships"

Alongside: the position of the ship when it is beside a peer or vessel

Amidships: the middle of the ship

Anchorage: the place where ships drop anchor. Also, a city in Alaska :-)

Astern: refers to something behind the ship

Berth: a built-in bunk bed. Can also refer to the ship's pier

Bow: the front of the ship

Bridge: the glassed in, raised area at the front of the ship where the captain works

Cabin: the room were you will sleep while onboard

Cabin steward: a housekeeping crew member who will attend to your state room

Course: the direction in which the ship is headed

Disembarkation: exiting or leaving the ship

Embarkation: entering or joining the ship

Fore: the front of the ship

Galley: the ship's kitchen

Gangway: the removable ramp that allows people to get on and off the ship

Head: the toilet

Hold: the cargo area below decks

Knot: one nautical mile per hour

Manifest: lists of the ship's entire passengers, crew, and cargo

Mess: where the crew members eat

Moor: to secure the ship in place with cables or anchors

Muster: to converge at your emergency lifeboat drill station

PAX: what crew members call passengers

Port agent: the person who gets you to the ship

Ports of call: the places where you will be stopping on your voyage

Port side: the left side of the ship when facing forward

Purser: the crew member in charge of passenger services

Shore excursion: local sightseeing tour's offered in ports of call

Stabilizer: the mechanisms that provide a smoother sailing experience

State room: a cruise ship cabin

Starboard: the right side of the ship when facing the bow, opposite the port side

Stern: the back or rear of the ship

Tender: a boat that transports passengers and supplies between ship and shore

Turnaround Day: transition day between voyages where new passengers get on

Weigh anchor: to raise the anchor out of the sea and set sail

At the Ice Bar in Auckland,
New Zealand

How to Pack for Your Cruise Ship Trip
(Without Checking Any Luggage)

A s I write this, I'm sitting in a hotel near the airport in Atlanta. I wasn't supposed to be here today but the winter storm that's raging through the Northeast caused many flight cancellations including mine.

I arrived in Atlanta only to find that my connecting flight had been cancelled and that I would have to find a hotel room for the night. Good thing I have an extra day to catch the ship!

I'm kicking myself right now because I checked my luggage.

I haven't checked a bag since I flew from Jamaica to Tokyo for a TV appearance. My luggage was put on the wrong plane and I almost had to go on the air with a borrowed suit that was about two sizes too big for me.

It ended up getting delivered to the studio about five minutes before we started shooting in front of a live audience, but I vowed never again to check my bags if I could help it.

This morning I forgot that lesson and now I'm left without a change of clothes, toiletries, or any of the work I was intending to do.

Don't let this happen to you!

The only way you can make sure this never happens is to carry on your luggage.

I could have carried my luggage on the plane this morning, it was small enough to fit in the overhead compartment, but I didn't. Maybe that was so I'd be inspired to write this carry-on packing list for you

How to Pack for Your Next Cruise Ship Trip Without Checking Any Luggage

1. Get luggage with a total dimension of 45"

Most airlines currently allow you to carry on 1 piece of luggage with a total length, width, and height of 45". So the first thing to do is make sure you have a suitcase that maxes out this limitation without exceeding it.

2. Get a catalogue case

Most airlines also allow you to carry on 1 personal item like a purse or a laptop bag. I carry a catalogue case. Airline pilots typically carry these for their flight manuals. They are big enough to store your laptop in the outer accordion compartment and then fill the inner compartment with clothes or shoes or toiletries or whatever didn't fit in your suitcase. Ladies can also stuff their purses into the center compartment of the catalogue case along with everything else.

3. Don't overpack

Almost everyone packs far more clothes than they need.
No matter where you are going, you can probably get by with:

- a single pair of jeans
- a single sweater
- a white dress shirt
- a dark pair of slacks
- a pair of sweatpants, shorts, and a bathing suit
- a few t-shirts (you'll buy more when you get there anyway)
- a dark suit and tie for men and a little black dress for women

4. Only pack two pairs of shoes and flip-flops

Men – a pair of sneakers and a pair of dress shoes.
Women – a pair of sneakers and a black pump with a low heel.

Trust me. It's enough.

4. Buy toiletries at your destination

They're cheap. They're easy to find. And not packing them will free up a lot of extra space in your luggage.

5. Only bring one book.

That's all you'll read anyway so why weigh yourself down with a lot of extra paper. Enjoy the change of scenery and save the book for the plane. If you want to bring more reading materials, then get yourself a digital book reader like the Amazon Kindle. It can hold over 1,000 books and fits in your jacket pocket.

6. Photocopy your important documents

Bring a copy of your Driver's License, Passport, and phone numbers for your Credit Card companies and leave it in the safe at your room. It can come in handy if your purse or wallet disappears.

7. Drop ship your books and CDs

Have your BOR products drop shipped directly to the port agent and they'll be waiting for you when you board the ship. This will save you from having to carry around an extra piece of luggage and since you're following my Cruise Ship Speaking System you'll be able to sell out of them on board and won't have to carry an empty suitcase home afterward!

8. Bring a laptop, noise canceling headphones, and an iPod or iPhone.

OK, so not everyone will need all of these, but they've become a must for me. I never travel without any of them. They help pass the time and provide a way to watch movies and listen to music while on long flights.

They also increase productivity. You can go through all of your email while on the plane without interruption. You can watch a seminar on your iPhone or listen to it on your iPod at the double speed setting while taking notes on your laptop. You can catch up on your work without your cellphone ringing or the Internet beckoning. You can get a lot done or if you just need a break from all that work, put on a sleep mask and some peaceful music and take a nice long nap.

The noise canceling headphones block out most of the ambient noise and the drone of the engine. I have the Bose QuietComfort headphones and they're amazing! I also recommend the $35 sleep mask from Brookstone that's filled with memory foam. It's like a puffy pillow for your eyes. Worth every penny.

In the atrium on a ship, on the way down to dinner

Cruise Ship Speaking Joshua Seth

Can't Sleep in Hotels?
Try This Travel Tip...

Here's a quick tip to help you get a better night's sleep in the hotel on the way to your next cruise ship speaking engagement or in your cabin while on board.

Did you ever notice that no matter how nice the hotel is, when you pull the certain closed there's always a gap between them. I'm on tour and in hotel rooms more often than I'm at home so I've encountered this annoyance hundreds of times. Light finds a way of streaming in through that little gap in the curtain, creating a slice of light through the room that always seems to lead directly to my eyes... as though the room had been designed specifically that way!

The welcoming committee in Cozumel, Mexico

After being woken up like this a few too many times, I devised a way to block out this early morning intruder once and for all. It's called a "Big Chip Clip". These are the little plastic clips that you can use to hold a half eaten bag of chips closed and wouldn't you know it, they work just as well on curtains too.

So on your next trip, toss one of those clips into your bag. Before you go to sleep that night use it to clip shut the curtains in your room. You'll get a much better night's sleep and not get woken up at the crack of dawn... unless you've got noisy neighbors. The clip only works well on them if you can get it to stay put on their mouths and I imagine it'd slip off pretty quickly... just prior to them chasing you down the hall in your PJs!

If you forget the clip you can always use one of the hangers in the room, the kind that has two clips on the bottom for holding a pair of pants or a skirt. Just turn the hanger sideways and use the two clips to clamp the curtain shut in the middle. It's better to bring the chip clip though because in some hotel rooms they've made it so you can't remove the hangers from the rods.

Sweet dreams! And make sure you set a wake up call so the total darkness doesn't seduce you into sleeping the day away.

Nighttime At Sea

Passport Information

S uccess starts with a commitment to take small decisive actions that lead to your goal. A great first step you can take today is to insure you have a valid and up to date passport. This is required before you can even set foot on a cruise ship.

Make sure you take care of this before you contact the cruise lines about speaking. It can take several weeks (4-6 weeks for a US Passport at the time of this writing) to get a passport, so if you don't have one already go ahead and apply for one right away.

Bookings can happen at any time and sometimes are at the very last minute. After all, you could get your first break as a fill-in for another presenter who has dropped out. The last thing you want is to have to turn down your first contract speaking on a cruise ship because your passport is out of date!

TIP: make sure you keep a copy of your passport with someone back home who can fax it to you if the need arises. I always carry a backup copy in my luggage as well.

Here's the webpage where you can find out how to apply for US passport, renew your existing passport, change the information on your passport, or replace a lost or stolen passport:

http://travel.state.gov/passport/passport_1738.html

You can also make an appointment at a regional passport office by calling 1-877-487-2778.

Here is where you can Apply for a Passport:

http://iafdb.travel.state.gov/

You may make an appointment to be seen at a Passport Agency only if:

- You need a U.S. passport in less than 2 weeks for international travel
- You need a U.S. passport within 4 weeks to obtain a foreign visa.

HERE IS A LIST OF ALL THE REGIONAL PASSPORT OFFICES IN THE US:

BOSTON Passport Agency
This Agency now issues the US Passport Card on-site!
Thomas P. O'Neill Federal Building
10 Causeway Street, Suite 247
Boston, MA 02222-1094
Hours: 8:30 a.m. - 4:30 p.m., local time, M-F, excluding Federal holidays
Automated Appointment Number: 1-877-487-2778

CHICAGO Passport Agency
This Agency now issues the US Passport Card on-site!
Kluczynski Federal Building
230 S. Dearborn Street, 18th Floor
Chicago, IL 60604-1564
Hours: 9:00 a.m. - 4:00 p.m., local time, M-F,
excluding Federal holidays
Automated Appointment Number: 1-877-487-2778

COLORADO Passport Agency
Cherry Creek III
3151 South Vaughn Way, Suite 600
Aurora, CO 80014
Hours: 8:00 a.m. - 3:00 p.m., local time,
M-F, excluding Federal holidays
Automated Appointment Number: 1-877-487-2778

CONNECTICUT Passport Agency
50 Washington Street
Norwalk, CT 06854
Hours: 9:00 a.m. - 4:00 p.m., local time, M-F,
excluding Federal holidays
Automated Appointment Number: 1 (877) 487-2778

DALLAS Passport Agency
This Agency now issues the US Passport Card on-site!
Earle Cabell Federal Building
1100 Commerce St, Suite 1120
Dallas, TX 75242
Hours: 8:00 a.m.- 3:00 p.m., local time, M-F,
excluding Federal holidays.
Inclement Weather: Listen to radio/TV
Automated Appointment Number: 1-877-487-2778

DETROIT Passport Agency

This Agency now issues the US Passport Card on-site!
211 West Fort Street, 2nd floor
Detroit, MI 48226-3269
Hours: 9:00 a.m.- 3:30 p.m., Local Time, M-F,
excluding Federal holidays
Automated Appointment Number: 1-877-487-2778

HONOLULU Passport Agency

Prince Kuhio Federal Building
300 Ala Moana Blvd., Suite 1-330
Honolulu, HI 96850
Hours: 8:30 a.m. - 3:00 p.m., local time, M-F,
excluding Federal holidays
Automated Appointment Number: 1 (877) 487-2778

HOUSTON Passport Agency

This Agency now issues the US Passport Card on-site!
Mickey Leland Federal Building
1919 Smith Street, 4th Floor
Houston, TX 77002-8049
Hours: 8:00 a.m. - 3:30 p.m., local time, M-F,
excluding Federal holidays
Automated Appointment Number: 1-877-487-2778

LOS ANGELES Passport Agency

Federal Building
11000 Wilshire Blvd.
Suite 1000
Los Angeles, CA 90024-3615
Hours: 7:00 a.m. - 3:00 p.m., local time, M-F,
excluding Federal holidays
Automated Appointment Number: 1-877-487-2778

MIAMI Passport Agency
This Agency now issues the US Passport Card on-site!
Omni Center
1501 Biscayne Boulevard, Suite 210
Miami, FL 33132
Hours: 8:00 a.m. - 3:00 p.m., local time, M-F,
excluding Federal holidays
Automated Appointment Number: 1-877-487-2778

MINNEAPOLIS Passport Agency
This Agency now issues the US Passport Card on-site!
212 South Third Avenue
Minneapolis, MN 55401
Hours: 8:30 a.m. to 3:00 p.m, local time, M-F,
excluding Federal holidays
Automated Appointment Number: 1-877-487-2778

NEW ORLEANS Passport Agency
One Canal Place (corner of Canal and North Peters Streets)
365 Canal Street, Suite 1300
New Orleans, LA 70130-6508
Hours: 8:00 a.m. - 12 p.m., local time, M-F,
excluding Federal holidays
Automated Appointment Number: 1-877-487-2778

NEW YORK Passport Agency
This Agency now issues the US Passport Card on-site!
Great New York Federal Building
376 Hudson Street
New York, NY 10014
Hours: 7:30 a.m. - 3:00 p.m., local time, M-F,
excluding Federal holidays
Automated Appointment Number: 1-877-487-2778

PHILADELPHIA Passport Agency
U.S. Custom House
200 Chestnut Street, Room 103
Philadelphia, PA 19106-2970
Hours: 8:00 a.m. - 3:00 p.m., local time, M-F,
excluding Federal holidays
Automated Appointment Number: 1-877-487-2778

SAN FRANCISCO Passport Agency
95 Hawthorne Street, 5th Floor
San Francisco, CA 94105-3901
Hours: 9:00 a.m. - 4:00 p.m., local time, M-F,
excluding Federal holidays
Automated Appointment Number: 1-877-487-2778

Th hat eating parrots of
Grand Cayman island!

SEATTLE Passport Agency
Henry Jackson Federal Building
915 Second Avenue, Suite 992
Seattle, WA 98174-1091
Hours: 8:00 a.m. - 3:00 p.m., local time,
M-F, excluding Federal holidays
Automated Appointment Number: 1-877-487-2778

WASHINGTON Passport Agency
1111 19th Street, N.W.
First Floor, Sidewalk Level
Washington, D.C. 20036
Hours: 8:00 a.m. - 3:00 p.m., local time, M-F,
excluding Federal holidays
Automated Appointment Number: 1 (877) 487-2778

WESTERN PASSPORT CENTER
Western Passport Center
7373 East Rosewood Street
Tucson, AZ 85710
Hours: 8:30 a.m. - 3:00 p.m., local time, M-F,
excluding Federal holidays
Automated Appointment Number: 1 (877) 487-2778

SPECIAL ISSUANCE Agency
1111 19th Street, N.W. Suite 200
Washington, D.C. 20036
Hours: 8:15 a.m. - 4:30 p.m., local time, M-F,
excluding Federal holidays

The famous windmills of Mykanos, Greece

The First Step To Creating Your Six Figure Speaking Business

What is your income goal for your speaking business this year?

Don't know? Then how will you achieve it? If you don't target a specific goal then how will you ever be able to hit it?

Take a minute right now and figure it out. What do you want to earn in your speaking business this year? And here's a little secret... that number is almost entirely based on your self-esteem. It's not the economy. It's not the market you're in. It's you.

The higher your self-esteem the more you'll think you deserve to make, the higher goals you'll set, and the easier it will be to take action to achieve those results. Many people will read this book but few will take action. Those that do are the one's that believe they deserve to be successful. Are you one of them? If so, then take a moment right now to write down your goals and make them that much closer to reality.

Whenever you define a goal and write it down you program it into your subconscious mind. You start a process that will set you on your way to the acquisition of that goal. As soon as you stop making excuses for not having, being, or doing everything you want in this life you will break right out of the prevailing zeitgeist of self-limiting beliefs and low expectations and you will create all the success you want in your career.

WRITE DOWN YOUR GOAL

The first step is to write down a number, a realistic income goal that you believe you can hit this year. There's no point in writing down "a million dollars" if you don't really believe that you can make that much this year. Write down a realistic income goal right now.

DO THE MATH

Good. Now divide that number by 12 and write that down underneath the larger number. That's what you'll need to make each and every month in order to hit your yearly income goal.

Now take that first, larger number and divide it by 50. Put that number last on your list. That's what you'll need to earn each and every week this year in order to make your stated income goal. So if you put down $100,000 and divided it by 50 you ended up with just $2,000 staring you in the face.

KICK IT UP A NOTCH

Seem realistic? Doable right now? Good. Then add 10% to that number. Just 10%. Now write it down.

See a lot of people set themselves up for failure by trying to hit goals that their mind hasn't grown into yet. They look around for that million dollar idea that will double or triple their income and end up chasing one pipe dream after another. This is a real shame when there are much easier ways to boost your income incrementally which will result in the same objective.

IMAGINE THIS…

What if, instead of seeking to double or triple your income this year you just resolved to book 10% more engagements. Just sold 10% more BOR at the end of your talks. And what if you sold them for 10% more then they're currently priced? Oh, and what if you started asking for and getting just 10% more referrals and repeat bookings than you do right now?

Are you starting to see how all these small improvements act as multipliers that can easily result in doubling or tripling your income without seeming unrealistic or overwhelming?

Now, take a look at your income goal that you wrote down a few moments ago. Would you like to increase it? Then cross it out. Just draw a big, bold like right through that number and write down your new accelerated income goal for the year. Circle it with a flourish and take it in.

PROJECT YOURSELF INTO THE FUTURE

Now take a moment and imagine that it's now the end of the year, you've done a few cruise ship gigs, built your client list, increased your product line and sales. See yourself having hit that income goal with confidence and ease. How does it feel? What does that scene look like in your mind? Who do you tell and how do they respond to your good news?

Guess what...

You're already on your way to making those dreams a reality. You've identified a realistic goal and visualized multiple ways of actually achieving it. You've written it down, emotionally committed to it, and visualized it actually happening. Now go one step further and post your new elevated income goal somewhere you can see it each and every day so you can keep your eye on the prize as you progress toward achieving it. Cruise ship speaking can help get you there but first you have to *believe* you can achieve it.

You can live your dreams and have a fulfilling life full of exciting adventures as a cruise ship speaker. You just have to take that first step and commit to doing it. And there's no time like the present.

We don't live forever you know. In fact, have you ever thought to count up the number of days you have to enjoy your life? How many do you think it is?

Millions of days? Hundreds of thousands of days? Tens of thousands of days?

Actually, you probably have less than 30,000 days to live (365 days x 80 years = 29,200 days). That's it. Then it's over.

How many have you used up already? How many have you squandered on unproven ideas that never panned out? How much longer are you willing to gamble with your future?

When I coach speakers and entertainers to improving their careers I usually find that they need to progress through the following steps first:

- Before you can live your dreams you need to identify what they are
- Before you can identify your dreams you need to believe that you are a person worth living them
- Before you can improve your self-esteem to the point where you can dream big dreams again, you need to take control of your life and stop allowing it to overwhelm you
- Before you can take control of your life, you need to learn certain skill-sets like stress reduction, time and information management, and simplicity of living
- Before you can do all that you need to change your mindset from one of reacting to your environment to one of proactively creating your environment

Wherever your career is at the moment, it is the cumulative result of all of your past thinking; therefore, you can change the course of your career and your life by changing your thinking now.

Look in the mirror before you go to bed tonight and say to yourself "I am a successful speaker." And really mean it. Substitute "I am a successful cruise ship speaker" if you like. Just do it with emotion and resolve. And repeat the process tomorrow morning and every morning and evening until it becomes your reality.

Don't skip that last tip. It's powerful and it works. Success starts and ends in your own mind. Make it work for you and give you the competitive edge to create your own six figure speaking business. You'll be glad you did.

Cruise Ship Speaking Joshua Seth

Cruise Line Contact Information

H ere is the contact information for the world's biggest cruise lines (the one's most likely to hire you as a cruise ship speaker). Use this contact information to request brochures, do research, and prepare yourself for the greatest adventure of your speaking career. Again, do not use it to pitch yourself as a presenter until after you have completed the Cruise Ship Speaking System. Keep your powder dry until you have a winning shot!

Carnival Cruises

888.carnival

3655 NW 87th Avenue
Miami, FL 33178

www.carnival.com

Carnival Cruise Lines prides itself on delivering fun, memorable vacations to our guests by offering a wide array of quality cruises which present outstanding value for the money. Our fleet of "Fun Ships" sails to more than 60 of the world's most beautiful destinations. Most stuff is already included on a Carnival cruise.

Because we think that when you sail with us, it's your time to let go and not worry about a thing. You'll visit amazing destinations and you only have to unpack once.

Celebrity Cruises
800-647-2251
1050 Caribbean Way
Miami, Fl 33132
www.celebritycruises.com

Our exceptional level of personal service, award-winning cuisine, world-famous amenities and accommodations that are the most spacious at sea, not only ensure an unforgettable cruise experience, but forge a lasting relationship between ourselves and our guests. It's no surprise that Celebrity guests and the travel press, such as Condé Nast Traveler, consistently rate Celebrity Cruises as one of the world's finest cruise lines. Experience for yourself what sets Celebrity apart.

Costa Cruises
877-88-COSTA
200 S Park Road, Suite 200
Hollywood FL 33021
www.costacruise.com

Each of Costa's ships has been designed in the style and traditions of Italy. These magnificent vessels, created to be among the most exciting and stunningly beautiful ships of our time, are floating palaces with every comfort, convenience and amenity offered for the enjoyment of their guests. Costa's ships feature millions of dollars in original works of art including sculptures, paintings, murals, wall hangings and hand-crafted artisan furnishings. Oversized staterooms, most of which feature ocean views and verandas offer their guests all the comforts of home.

Cruise West
888-851-8133
2301 Fifth Avenue, Suite 401
Seattle, WA 98121-1856
www.cruisewest.com

Cruise West is a second-generation, family-owned company that enables travelers to explore remote locales not accessible to larger cruise ships. Cruise West's smaller ships hold only 78-138 guests, encouraging congenial interaction between guests and crew and creating a relaxed environment. All ships have forward lounges and ample outdoor deck space for viewing and photographing wildlife and scenery. All vessels are also equipped with inflatable landing craft for up-close exploration of remote areas and shore landings.

Crystal Cruises
888-722-0021
2049 Century Park East, Suite 1400
Los Angeles, CA 90067
www.crystalcruises.com

At Crystal Cruises, we are motivated by a single goal: to provide you with the finest experience not only in cruising, but in all of luxury travel. Aboard the two highest-rated ships in the world, Crystal Symphony and Crystal Serenity, you will discover the hallmarks of Crystal... extraordinary service, abundant space, exceptional quality and incredible choices. This is the very essence of our company; this is the Crystal Difference. A steadfast commitment to excellence has earned us unprecedented recognition as the World's Best for an incredible 15 years – an accomplishment unmatched by any other cruise line, hotel or resort anywhere in the world.

Cunard Line Ltd.

800-728-6273

www.cunardline.com

For over a century and a half, the iconic ships of Cunard have been defining sophisticated ocean travel. They have always been The Most Famous Ocean Liners In The World®. From her fabled vessels of the past to her present royal court — Queen Mary 2, Queen Victoria and our newest Ocean Liner, Queen Elizabeth— Cunard has carried guests across the great oceans and to the far points of the globe in unparalleled style.

Disney Cruise Line

951-3532

P.O. Box 10238
Lake Buena Vista, FL 32830-0238

www.disneycruise.com

Disney Cruise Line offers a vacation experience unlike any other that magically brings families together while still providing kid and adult-only time that caters to their unique needs. Discover what makes a Disney cruise a one-of-a-kind voyage that includes the attention to detail, world-class hospitality and legendary service that Disney is famous for—and that only Disney could provide.

Cruise Ship Speaking   Joshua Seth

Fred Olsen Cruises

44 (0) 1473-746175

Fred. Olsen House
White House Road
Ipswich, Suffolk, IP1 5LL

www.fredolsencruises.com

Fred. Olsen Cruise Lines has defined and refined the cruise experience, and judging by the number of passengers that come back time and again, we seem to have styled it to perfection.

Holland America Line

877-932-4259

Holland America Line
300 Elliott Ave. West
Seattle, WA 98119

www.hollandamerica.com

For more than 136 years, Holland America Line has been a recognized leader in cruising, taking our guests to exotic destinations around the world. If you are looking for some of the most spacious and comfortable ships at sea, award-winning service, five star dining, extensive activities and enrichment programs and compelling worldwide itineraries, you've come to the right place. Holland America Line's fleet of 14 elegant, mid-size ships offers nearly 500 sailings a year visiting all seven continents.

Norwegian Cruise Lines

866-234-7350

7665 Corporate Center Drive
Miami, Florida 3312

www.ncl.com

There's a big difference between NCL and other cruise lines. We call it Freestyle Cruising. You'll find it in the flexible cruise vacations we offer our guests. You'll feel it in the dedication and passion of our team members. You'll see it in our commitment to the environment. The Freestyle spirit is part of everything we do. Sound good? Then you're probably a lot like one of our customers - people who like to go their own way.

Oceania Cruises

800-531-5619

8300 NW 33rd Street, Suite 308
Miami, Florida 33122

www.oceaniacruises.com

Oceania Cruises is the world's largest upper premium cruise line. The finest cuisine at sea, award-winning itineraries and outstanding value define Oceania Cruises' five-star product and have positioned the company as the cruise line of choice for travelers seeking a truly refined and casually elegant travel experience. Our three intimate and luxurious 684-guest ships allow you to explore the world in unequalled style and comfort. Oceania Cruises sails to more than 180 ports in Europe, China and the Far East, Australia, New Zealand, South America, Central America and the Caribbean. Featuring three intimate and elegant mid-sized ships, Regatta, Insignia and Nautica, the line will introduce two new mid-size Oceania-Class ships to its award-winning fleet in 2010 and 2011.

Cruise Ship Speaking   Joshua Seth

P&O Cruises

0845-678-00-14

Carnival House
100 Harbour Parade
Southampton SO15 1ST

www.pocruises.com

If you want your holiday to be extraordinary, you've come to the right place. Choose P&O Cruises and the extraordinary happens every day. Imagine awaking to a new view each morning. Enjoying service that is unlike anything on land. Visiting more beautiful and vibrant places in one holiday than most people see in years. Dining in exclusive restaurants. Doing what you want, when you want.

Princess Cruises

800-774-6237

24844 Avenue Rockefeller
Santa Clarita, CA 91355

www.princess.com

One of the best-known names in cruising, Princess Cruises first set sail in 1965 with a single ship cruising to Mexico. Today, the line has grown to become the third largest cruise line in the world, renowned for innovative ships, an array of onboard options, and an environment of exceptional customer service. A recognized leader in worldwide cruising, Princess offers approximately 1.3 million passengers each year the opportunity to escape to the top destinations around the globe, aboard a fleet of 18 modern vessels.

Silver Sea Line

110 East Broward Blvd
Fort Lauderdale, FL 33301

Phone: 800.722.9955

www.silversea.com

Sumptuous ocean-view suites and the luxurious freedom of an all-inclusive lifestyle. Distinctive European styling reflected in every detail, from uncompromising service to exquisite gourmet dining. The convivial ambience of intimate spaces and well-travelled international guests. Exotic destinations, exclusive explorations, and uniquely enriching cultural connections. This is the secret allure of ocean travel. This is Silversea.

Regent Seven Seas Cruises

877-505-5370

1000 Corporate Drive, Suite 500
Fort Lauderdale, Florida 33334

www.rssc.com

The ships of Regent Seven Seas Cruises offer voyages of exploration and discovery to more than 300 ports on all seven continents. Our luxury vessels are designed for guests numbering in the hundreds rather than the thousands. The ambiance on board is personal, individual, accommodating - "upscale but not uptight." And all ships share certain distinctions in accommodations, service, dining and amenities that elevate them to the lofty vantage point of our enviable six stars.

Royal Caribbean

866-562-7625

1050 Caribbean Way
Miami, FL 33132-2096

www.royalcaribbean.com

Royal Caribbean's cruise ships are the most innovative and exciting in the travel industry. From rock-climbing walls on every ship, to elegant dining rooms and relaxing spas, your experience onboard is nothing short of incredible. And the service you get will be just as amazing, with our signature Gold Anchor ServiceSM on every ship.

*At the opera house in
Sydney, Australia*

Stories From
The 7 Seas: Italy

As I write this, I've just returned from a series of cruise ship gigs in Italy. One of the great things about presenting on cruise ships is that you often get the opportunity to travel to the same destinations more than once. So while everyone else is running around trying to squeeze Rome into a day, you can pick and choose your adventures, knowing that you'll soon return for more.

After having sailed up the Italian coastline so many times I've been able to distill some of the high points of these ports of call. So here's what to do the next time you're speaking on a cruise to Italy:

Venice – It's beautiful, it's small, it's sinking, and contrary to popular belief it's not stinking. The water smells nice actually, but I still wouldn't drink it. Take the water taxi through the Grand Canal instead of dropping a hundred euros for a much shorter trip in a gondola. It may not be quite as romantic, but you'll see much more of the city and have all that money left over for an intimate dinner overlooking the Doge's Palace in San Marco square afterward.

Naples – The birthplace of pizza, the mafia, and Sophia Loren. That's everything you need to know, now get out of town and go see Pompeii or Capri! Did I mention they have great pizza? The best pizza I've ever had in my life was in a little roadside stand just opposite the entrance to the ruins at Pompeii. Take the train up from the port area and have one before you explore the ruins. You'll work up an appetite hiking all over that once buried city, which is great, because that means you'll have room for another incredible pizza before heading back to the ship!

Pisa – Skip it. Just photoshop yourself into a picture where you look like you're holding up the leaning tower. No need to actually go there. Better to head a little further up the road to Florence. If you do stop in Pisa though, make sure you go inside the church that's next to that famous tower. It's has some amazing artwork inside and most people miss it.

Florence – The entire city is like a gigantic Renaissance art and sculpture museum. You can walk around all day taking pictures of famous statues on display in pretty much every intersection and square. They also have the best gelato in all of Italy!

Rome - One of the most amazing cities in the history of the world. Deserves more than a day. Put it on your "must see before I die" list. It's a ways from the port though so this would be the time to join an organized tour. If you're adventurous though, you can take the train from the station which is a short walk from the port. Highlights include: the Colosseum, the Vatican, the Pantheon, the Forum, the Spanish Steps, and the incomparable Trevi Fountain.

The Complete Cruise Ship Speaking System

B y now you realize what a wonderful opportunity awaits you as
a cruise ship speaker. The travel, the adventure, and the business
building opportunities are unparalleled in the speaking industry.
Never before have there been so many luxury cruise ships in need of
so many speakers. You could be one of them.

But there's no time to wait. As more and more speakers discover the
benefits of adding the cruise ship market to their professional resumes
the competition for these gigs will heat up. Booking these gigs may
still be relatively easy, but it won't always be that way.

I want to give you everything you need to know to book these gigs
and use them to build a six figure speaking business back on land.
There's a lot more valuable information than would fit between the
covers of this book. Some things you just have to see and hear for
yourself. That's why I've developed the complete "Cruise Ship
Speaking System", a collection of 10 CDs and DVDs that will guide
you step-by-step toward becoming the most successful cruise ship
speaker you can be.

YOUR STEP-BY-STEP SYSTEM INCLUDES:

CD 1: Quickstart Introduction To Get You Up And Running Right Away

CD 2: How To Get Your First Booking (a step by step strategy to becoming a cruise ship speaker)

CD 3: How To Create A Great Cruise Ship Lecture The Fast And Easy Way

CD 4: How To Get Shore Excursions Worth Hundreds of Dollars For Free

CD 5: Backstage Interviews With Cruise Ship Speakers

CD 6: Speaker's Reveal: Travel Lessons Learned The Hard Way So You Don't Have To

CD 7: How To Run Your Speaking office At Sea

DVD 8: Powerfully Profitable BOR Sales Strategies (Specific To Cruise Ships)

DVD 9: Q&A Interviews With Agents and More

DVD 10: Insiders Tips and MoneySaving Secrets Exclusively for Cruise Ship Speakers

That's 10 discs in all that cover everything from how to get the gigs to how to prepare for them to how to turn them into turn-key money making machines. Many of these recordings were made right on cruise ships so it's like you're right there on board with me while I walk you through everything you need to know before you go.

There has never been so much inside information available to the professional speaker about this incredibly fun and profitable hidden speaking market. I've given you everything you need to not only get these gigs but to profit from them immediately. I personally left a lot of money on the table because I had to figure this stuff out bit by bit over the course of several years. I want you to know everything from the get-go. What took me over three years and a lot of trial and error to learn is now yours for the taking.

As A Special Bonus For Readers Of This Book...

I'll personally help you prepare for success on the high seas with a free phone consultation. In this call you can have any of your most important speaking questions answered. My coaching clients pay me up to $500 for private coaching calls. You'll get it free. Just put the word "bookbonus" into the the coupon code box when you order your complete Cruise Ship Speaking System through this page:

www.CruiseShipSpeaking.com/specialoffer

There are literally thousands of speaking engagements available on cruise ships each and every year. And you know what? On some of these cruises they're actually scrambling to get the speakers. Last summer, when the gas prices were so high, they didn't have enough speakers to go on some of the European cruises. The European speakers didn't want to drive down to meet the ship because the cost of the petrol was so high. So there were actually cruises leaving the ports to go on fantasy 12-day vacations to Italy and the Greek Isles *with no cruise ship speakers on board* and it could have been you. Should have been you. And that's why I say…do not wait. The time is now.

Get the complete Cruise Ship Speaking System and start your new life of travel and adventure today. Your speaking career has never been so much fun!

About the Author

Joshua Seth is a Certified Hypnotist (CHt) with the National Guild of Hypnotists and is the author of the book "The Weight Loss Hypnosis Solution: How to lose weight permanently without diets or willpower."

HIs weight loss hypnosis seminars on cruise ships have attracted over 40,000 participants and he now coaches other speakers to duplicate his success.

As a stage hypnotist he has been called "Amazingly Captivating" by American Entertainment Magazine, "The #1 American Hypnotist" by TV Japan, and "The Rock Star of Hypnosis" by Campus Activities Magazine who also declares he has "A High Energy, One-Of-A-Kind Show."

Over 250,000 people have now seen Joshua live and millions more have experienced him through his two Japanese television specials.

Even if you've never seen Joshua perform live, you've heard his voice as the starring role of "Tai" on the #1 Saturday morning cartoon "Digimon", the starring role of "Tetuso" in the anime classic Akira, and over 50 other TV Shows and Movies (including various roles in the Spongebob Squarepants Movie).

Joshua is a Hollywood Academy of Magical Arts Award Winner and has been featured on the WB, ABC Family, The CW, the Discovery Channel, and Fox.

To inquire about having Joshua speak and perform at your conference, bootcamp, or seminar email info@joshuaseth.com

In Paris at The Eiffel Tower
(where Suzy and I got engaged
between cruise ship gigs)

At the beach in Gran Turk

Put music actively in
y life
Do you really listen
to the message of song?
Hear it! Sing it,
Live it

as you own ministery
+ message for living the
remainder of y life (what
ever time + life you
may have remaing in
your world)
We each do have our
own world — especially our
inner self talk + what
We accept about ourself
+ others especially those
We admire + love,
Listen — meditate — love
"Don't die w/y music
still inside you" + Act.

12161369R10076

Made in the USA
Lexington, KY
02 December 2011